Why Did God Make Zits & Other Disgusting
Stuff?

Why Did GOD Make Zits & Other Disgusting Stuff?

Questions Preteens Ask

KEL GROSECLOSE

DIMENSIONS
FOR LIVING

NASHVILLE

WHY DID GOD MAKE ZITS AND OTHER DISGUSTING STUFF?

This book is printed on acid-free, recycled paper.

Library of Congress Cataloging-in-Publication Data

Groseclose, Kel, 1940–
  Why did God make zits and other disgusting stuff?: questions preteens
ask / Kel Groseclose.
    p. cm.
  ISBN 0-687-46586-9 (alk. paper)
    1. Children—United States—Miscellanea. 2. Child psychology—United States—
Miscellanea. 3. Children—United States—Religious life—Miscellanea. I. Title.
HQ792.U5G74 1993
305.23—dc20   92-47417

Scripture quotations are from the New Revised Standard Version Bible, copyright © 1989, by the Division of Christian Education of the National Council of the Churches of Christ in the U.S.A. Used by permission.

93 94 95 96 97 98 99 00 01 02—10 9 8 7 6 5 4 3 2 1

MANUFACTURED IN THE UNITED STATES OF AMERICA

Posthumously dedicated to Harrell Beck, beloved professor at Boston University School of Theology, who in life was a treasure of gentle wisdom for me; who in death has enriched and given new meaning to the "fellowship of the saints." When I need inspiration or courage, Harrell's spirit comes winging its way to me.

CONTENTS

Contents

INTRODUCTION

Whew! Double whew! The youth room at the church was a zoo with eleven active, excited, and loud young people who were bored even before the first month of summer vacation was over. They'd gathered on a warm July evening to share with me the questions in their hearts and minds. After I'd established a semblance of order (no small task) and explained what I was hoping to accomplish, the questions came from those young persons as rapidly as popcorn at its peak of popping.

I couldn't write fast enough to keep pace. Two hours later, they were still going strong. I'd scribbled more than ten pages of notes. A few questions were of the off-the-wall variety and several were ones I dared not repeat, the kind that are accompanied by nervous giggles. Along with the predictably silly questions came dozens upon dozens of profound inquiries. If these eleven are like other young people in the world, and I'm certain they are, then an entire library shelf could be filled with books on the important questions they raise. The process got me enthused for the task of writing. Thankfully, someone in the group saved the best question for last. "Where's the ice cream you promised us?"

God probably wouldn't mind if we added one more Beatitude to the nine that Jesus spoke in the Sermon on the Mount. Right after "Blessed are the pure in heart, for they will see God" (Matthew 5:8), we'll slip in "Blessed are those who ask questions, for they will grow spiritually by leaps and bounds."

God has placed a natural and delightful curiosity within the spirit of every human being from innocent little children to wrinkled senior citizens. A special place is reserved for preteens and young adults. Asking questions is a gift of the Spirit, a divine blessing, a godly inspiration. Searching, seeking, investigating and inquiring are essential ingredients in the process of gaining wisdom. There's a catch, however. After we ask, we need to listen and then accept the answers as they begin to form.

Questioning is not a sign of rebelliousness. Far from it! Asking questions offers wonderful possibilities for intellectual, emotional, and spiritual growth. People in positions of authority—parents, teachers, pastors, politicians, law enforcement officers, and others—ought to be on friendly terms with that squiggle with a dot at the bottom. It provides opportunities for them to share their views, opinions, and beliefs.

Young people must pry and poke and challenge to search for truth. They must sort out the legacy from their elders, separate the wheat from the chaff, and discern what's worth retaining and what should be discarded. Perceptive questions serve as the mileposts along a preteen's journey toward maturity.

The preteen and early teen years are perfect for questioning, for asking about everything and anything. People at that age don't yet "owe their soul to the company store" and usually have fewer commitments and responsibilities, permitting a greater degree of freedom for exploration.

Although it's definitely a time of transition, adolescence has value in and of itself. A certain amount of growing pains is to be expected. But adolescence is not simply to be endured until something better comes along. It can be a very positive and productive stage in a person's life. Young people have unique gifts and graces to offer to their families, to their friends, and to the whole world.

Without exception, the significant questions we humans ask must be addressed by the entire community. One individual, no matter how clever and wise, cannot possibly provide complete, satisfying answers. Family discussions, classes, church youth groups, Bible study gatherings, or even lunch in the school cafeteria can be settings for wrestling with the issues on our minds. As we seek and struggle in concert with one another, fresh ideas will emerge. When we share questions and insights, our powers of imagination are greatly enhanced, and our inner vision improves immeasurably.

Adolescents are as diverse as any other age group. Each youth is a one-of-a-kind individual. Some will be veritable bundles of bewilderment and will place question marks at the end of nearly every sentence. Others may be far less vocal but quietly wonder about the same thing. People at every stage in life are inquisitive creatures. The questions may vary, but the seeking and wondering remain constant.

Praise God for unanswered questions! They indicate that there's room for growth; that life's open-ended; that faith is an ongoing, continuing quest. Truth, therefore, isn't something one generation can package and hand all neat and tidy to succeeding generations. Truth is very democratic and shows absolutely no favoritism. It visits whomever it chooses from tiny babes to the most ancient of souls.

While this book is written in language that speaks directly to preteens and younger youth, parents and other adults will also benefit from reading the various chapters. It could prove helpful in opening channels of communication between adolescents and adults, in encouraging a clarification of beliefs and values, and in assisting persons of different generations to understand more clearly one another's views. In addition, a number of the questions addressed might be useful for youth groups and classes as a supplement to basic curricula and as discussion starters on key issues.

My deep appreciation goes to the staff at Wenatchee First United Methodist Church for providing me with a quiet place and an endless supply of coffee. My special thanks to Mary

Gates for her insights and honest but gracious appraisal. Finally, I could not have managed without the input, energy, and intelligent questions of those eleven young people— Stephen Wallace, Jim Rainbolt, Dana Mead, Paige Ahnemiller, Erin Wallace, Betsy Morris, Caryn Twombly, Josh Closser, Eric G. Dull, Jeff L. Thomas, and David Twombly.

As you read these pages, I hope you are challenged and blessed by them as much as I was in creating them.

Kel Groseclose
Wenatchee, Washington

1

Where Do I Grow from Here?

These are the best of times to be a young person. Yes, I know, the human race is facing more problems than ever before; millions of people are homeless and billions are hungry. Violence is an all too common occurrence. And there's certainly no shortage of "gloomsters and doomsters" predicting terrible tragedies in our immediate future, up to and including the end of the world. Yet in the history of this planet, the possibilities for wonderful, positive, good things to happen have never been greater.

I'm going to jump up and down and throw a mini-fit of frustration if I hear one more adult say, "I'm sure glad my children are grown. I wouldn't want to have the responsibility of raising kids in this rotten world." Okay, so it's not perfect. But since it's all we've got at the moment, we'd better make the best of it.

Perhaps you think I'm a bit wacky for beginning a book with a chapter on the future. You say logic suggests it should come at the end? Well, I like it right where it is because the rest of the questions in this book are about the future. This isn't a history book, although with a title that has the word *zits* in it, you probably figured that out! The point is that all of us need to be forward-looking people, amateur futurists if you will.

We're in an age of worldwide transition. Many old patterns simply won't fit the emerging ways of the twenty-first century. By the time you are in your early twenties, our planet will greet a new decade, a new century, and a new millennium all at the same time. Changing millennia is quite rare; by definition it occurs only once every thousand years.

Historical transitions are tough because there's nobody to tell us exactly what to do. Nobody who saw the last millennium is still around. That means we're on our own; it's up to us. That can be a little scary. What if we mess up? On the other hand, these are very exciting times. We have a rare opportunity to make a fresh start for the world—a chance to explore new possibilities, to strike out in different directions. We're free to experiment. So we make a few mistakes—or even a lot. Big deal. The greatest accomplishments of the human race have always involved taking risks.

This era may have remarkable similarities to the first century. We might well be feeling much like the original twelve disciples felt after Jesus' crucifixion and resurrection. What do we do now? they wondered as they huddled together in the upper room. They didn't want to go home and back to their old jobs, but they were uncomfortable about moving into an uncertain future. I can imagine their conversation with God.

"This is God speaking."

"Who?"

"God! You remember me? I'm the Creator, the One who spoke to the prophets, inspired David to write psalms, and sent my Son Jesus to live with you and teach you my will."

"Oh, yeah, we remember now. We sort of forgot for a moment. Sorry. Please forgive us. We're still a little rattled. A lot's happened to us lately, you know."

"I know. My, do I ever know! Listen, I have a plan I'd like to try on you. I want you to start the Church. What do you say?"

"Maybe we could; but what's a *church?*"

"It's a group of people who love me, follow Jesus, and want to help others. My risen Son will be the head of the whole operation. I promise to send my Spirit to give you guidance and strength. How does that sound?"

"Not bad for starters. Peter wants to know who gets to be the bishop?"

"Who said anything about bishops?"

Like those disciples of old, we disciples today are living in stressful times. Yet there have never been more creative possibilities. God's grace is a powerful reality. The potential for positive things to occur is incredible. Global communications permit us to share information instantly with all other peoples on the earth. Medical advances give us the hope of providing healthy lives for children and adults everywhere. Agricultural technology enables us to offer food to the world's hungry people. More people than ever before live in freedom and dignity.

In order to maximize these opportunities in the new millennium, we'll need a number of important qualities—for instance, courage. We're being asked by God to move into uncharted territory. It's not an assignment for the timid or faint of heart. Maybe we'll do a lot of whistling in the dark and taking little baby steps. That's to be expected. I personally would like someone with whom to hold hands during our journey into the future.

We'll also need an ample supply of patience. No matter what age you are, waiting is hard work. But God will unfold this new world according to God's own timetable. Our duty is to be alert and ready to respond, to be watching for God to give us clues.

Then there's trust. When it feels as if we're lost in the wilderness; when we feel frightened, lonely, and tired; that's when we've got to trust God. God brought the Hebrews through the desert into the Promised Land. Okay, it took forty long and difficult years. But they made it. God will surely bring us safely into this beautiful new world that awaits us.

The question remains: Where do we grow from here? To be partners with God in creating something special and unique means we must grow spiritually, mature in our faith, deepen our love, and increase our commitment. Are you ready?

2

Where in the World Is God?

I t was a struggling church youth group made up mostly of new members. They'd tried a number of gimmicks to increase attendance—pizza parties, bowling nights, dances, and games. It was working, but they felt something important was missing. One particular Sunday evening the adult leader, Caitlin, surprised everybody. "I have homework for you this week—a written assignment."

"No way," said Jake coming half out of his seat. "I have to study at school. I'm here for the fellowship and fun, and nobody can make me do homework for a youth group."

"Yeah," Aimee added. "I already have too many tests and papers to do. I don't need any more, that's for sure."

"Hold on, mellow out," replied Caitlin. "This isn't a 'have-to.' I was hoping it would be a 'want-to.' Anyway, how can you make up your minds so quickly? You don't even know what I was going to suggest."

"So go ahead and tell us. But we'll probably still say 'forget it,' " Jake said.

"Okay, here's the plan. For the next week I'd like each of you to keep a diary of the . . ."

"Hold it right there," interrupted Jeremy. "Men don't keep diaries; we make journal entries."

"I stand corrected. As I was saying, keep a journal of where you see God in the world—a record of the places you find God at work, of the people who reveal God to you, of those times when you feel very close to God. Does that make sense?"

"I suppose so," Alberto answered. "How long does it have to be? You know, how many pages? Do we have to type it? And are you going to give us a grade?"

"I don't care if you scribble words on a napkin as long as you can read your own writing. And no, I'm not going to grade anything. This project is just for you. However, next Sunday I'd like you to share whatever insights you've gained. Is that agreeable with everybody?"

The entire group groaned, "We guess so."

Time flew by as it usually does when you're super busy. Suddenly it was Sunday again. Chris was supposed to do the devotion but had forgotten. Well, he admitted he hadn't actually forgotten. He couldn't think of anything to do. His mind had drawn a total blank.

"No problem," Caitlin offered. "Let's sing a couple of our favorite songs, and I'll lead a prayer." After the "amen," Jake raised his hand. "Yes, Jake, do you have something to share?"

"I do. You remember how I didn't want to keep that journal in the first place? Well, I changed my attitude. It happened on Tuesday. My buddies and I were walking home when we saw this grubby-looking man. He was hunched over, his toes were sticking out of his shoes, he hadn't shaved in days, and he smelled to high heaven. The other guys started yelling at him—you know, making fun of him—saying stuff like 'Hey, old duffer, you stink so bad a skunk would hold its nose.' When I looked into his eyes, they were so sad something happened inside me. I told my friends to knock it off. They grumbled, but they quit. The man's face got this little smile on it, his eyes brightened, and he said, 'Thank you, young man.' It made me feel good all over. Suddenly, right there on the street corner I felt very close to God. Kind of silly, huh?"

"Kind of wonderful, I'd say," spoke up Kathy. Everyone else nodded in agreement.

"I had a similar experience," reported Peter. "On Thursday night, I had plans to watch a video at Melissa's, but my folks made me babysit my little sister. I call her 'The Pest' for obvious reasons. I stomped around the house, slammed a few doors, and performed your basically immature behavior. 'The Pest' wanted to see a Disney movie so I put it in the VCR. Then she wanted some popcorn, next a drink, and finally her Cabbage Patch Kid, which is the ugliest doll I've ever seen. I was sitting there angry at the whole world when she ran up, jumped on my lap, gave me a big hug, and said, 'You're my best big brother. I love you!' She planted a sloppy kiss on my face, hopped down, and roared off, leaving me with a sweet, warm feeling inside, sort of a glow. I couldn't figure out what was going on until this tiny voice in my head said, 'Peter, that was God.' If you'd have told me I'd find God by babysitting 'The Pest,' I'd have said you're as wacky as they come. But I did."

Mary Margaret was the next to share. "I was standing in line at a fast-food restaurant and had been waiting for an eternity. Maybe the food was fast, but the people serving it were slower than a snail on glue. There was a family behind me with a bunch of small kids who were trying to behave. But they were hungry and tired. It made me remember what it was like when I was their age and had to wait. I was suddenly overcome with compassion. When it was finally my turn, I stepped aside and asked them to go ahead. The parents were relieved and very appreciative. The children jumped for joy. Such a little thing to do, yet it produced such a neat feeling in me. I silently offered a prayer of thanksgiving to God for the happiness of serving others."

Caitlin suggested the group should silently join in Mary Margaret's prayer.

"This is an exciting evening! Who else would like to share?" Caitlin asked. Several hands shot up. "Alberto, why don't you go next?"

"I didn't exactly find God this week," he began, "God found me. Isn't that what we've all been saying?"

Everyone nodded.

"I was watching the news," continued Alberto, "and God was there on television. Hard to believe, huh? The report was about a devastating typhoon and flood in an Asian nation and it showed thousands upon thousands of homeless and grieving people. I cried, I couldn't help it. I don't think I've cried since I fell off a swing when I was five years old. But there I was, watching the TV with tears running down my cheeks. I saw God in those hurting people. As I cried I felt God tugging at my heart, asking me to do something to help. I decided to recycle aluminum cans, newspapers, and glass for the next month and give what I earn to the church's mission fund."

"Maybe our youth group could help you with your project," suggested David. "We'll talk about it during our business meeting." It was obvious that Rosa had something to say. She was perched on the edge of her chair. "I'd like to tell you guys and gals what happened at lunch. I always sit at the same table with my best friends. On Thursday I was late, so they saved me a spot. I got my food, but for some reason, I just waved at them and walked right on by. I felt as though somebody was leading me, directing my steps. I sat down at the table where the school's losers eat—you know, the ones who dress weird, the dorks and nerds, the loners and newcomers.

"It was awkward at first. They probably figured I was up to something. Gradually, though, we began to talk. I shared my piece of cake with a girl who doesn't speak English very well. Was she ever pleased when I got the courage to try my Spanish! Even though I messed up every other sentence, she didn't mind. We were communicating! Before the hour was over, we agreed to eat lunch together every day. I'll help her polish her English, and she'll help me learn Spanish. My other friends are really ticked off, but they'll come around. I'm hoping to get them to split up and sit at other tables, too. Who else but God could have made me leave the security of my old relationships and risk making a fool out of myself?"

"Have any of you noticed what time it is?" asked Caitlin. "We're already ten minutes late. We'll continue this discussion next week, I promise. Would anybody be willing to bring refreshments?"

Jake stood up and said, "No, but I'll do the devotion." The group was shocked. Nobody ever volunteered to do the devotion. "I already have an idea," he continued. "Would everybody please read Matthew 25 in preparation?"

The brief business meeting was the best they'd ever had. No one suggested they plan another trip to the bowling alley or the skating rink. Instead they talked about ways to serve the community. They decided to invite a representative from Habitat for Humanity to visit in a month; to start collecting canned goods for a food bank; to go Christmas caroling to the church's shut-ins, to the hospital, and maybe even to prisoners at the county jail.

As they formed their closing circle, Caitlin noted what a great evening it had been and how proud she was of them. "Doesn't God have wonderful surprises for us? Keep looking. But now you better hustle. Your parents are probably waiting. Have fun trying to explain to them what we've been up to tonight." Everybody gave an extra-hard squeeze to the hands they were holding.

3

Is It Okay to Sit on My Mom's Lap When I'm Taller Than She Is?

What a lap Sara's mom had! It was a world-class, gold-medal, super-duper lap. She could balance a dinner plate heaped with food, a water glass filled to the brim, a knife, fork, spoon, and napkin, plus a bowl of jello all at once on her lap. And the jello didn't even quiver! She had room for three cats, one kitten, and Max, the old family hound. What an amazing lap! When she sat in her favorite chair, she often held a big thick novel, her reading glasses, a soft drink, and a bowl overflowing with buttered popcorn; and still there was room for Max to squeeze in. No doubt about it, Sara's mom was a gifted woman.

But there was one very important thing her lap could no longer embrace: Sara. Something happened the year Sara turned twelve. She grew. Well, she didn't actually grow; she sprouted like Jack's famous beanstalk; she shot up like a skyscraper until she was taller than her mom. For that matter, she was taller than her daddy, too. She was an elegant, strikingly beautiful young woman. But fold them however she might, her long legs and arms simply could not and would not fit on her mom's lap anymore.

Through the years that lap had performed miracles for Sara. It had been her primary source of comfort. She'd taken countless naps there. When she was enfolded safely and securely, the troubles of the big world simply vanished. A few minutes of holding and *poof*—her cares and woes were gone for good. It was a magical, mystical lap. Snuggling there was better than hiding in the tree house halfway up the red maple in the front yard; better than visiting in a friend's playhouse when rain pitter-pattered on the roof; better than roasting marshmallows over red-hot coals in Grandma and Grandpa's rock fireplace.

Sara had bundles of happy memories from curling up in that lap. When she was a wee little thing, she'd take her bath, get her clean "jammies" on, and climb on Mom's lap for a special story time. It was a perfect fit, sort of a custom-designed recliner, only much warmer and softer. In fact, Mom's lap could hold four or more children at once. There was always room for everybody. No one was ever left out. Somehow Mom could peek around all those heads to see the words. Sara usually got to turn the pages.

When Sara was seven she had a major bicycle wreck. She skinned her knees, scraped the palms of both hands, cut her elbow, and bent her bike into a pretzel. It was a sad day for Sara. But after receiving a ton of sympathy while sitting on Mom's lap, and after Dad and his wrench managed to twist her bike back to its original shape (almost), the world seemed brighter and her scrapes and scratches didn't hurt so much.

On the day Grandma died, Sara knew right where to go. She made a beeline for Mom's lap, and together they comforted each other. Rocking in a high-backed chair, they were a duet of tears and laughter as they remembered how much Grandma had meant to them and how wonderful she was. It was a healing moment for both Sara and her mom.

So what do you think? Are you ever too old or too big to need the support and love of other people? No! A thousand, million, trillion times, no! You may be too tall or too wide to fit on somebody else's lap, that's true. But you and I don't ever outgrow our need to feel safe and secure, to know that we're loved all the way down to the tips of our big toes. This is true for boys and men as well as for girls and women. I've learned from experience that we all need the tenderness of touch and the joy of holding.

I was the ripe old age of forty before I completely learned this lesson. A high school student was my teacher. The youth group had attended a movie with a moving, emotional ending. When we returned to the church for a discussion and hot chocolate, I couldn't find Darren. I searched the building from top to bottom, but he was nowhere to be found. As I headed back to the youth room, I heard a noise in the sanctuary choir loft. Darren was sitting there in the dark, quietly crying. I started to leave, but he motioned for me to stay. Before long, we had our arms around each other's shoulders and were both crying. I still wonder what everybody else thought when we came back with our eyes puffy and red, our noses sniffling a mile a minute.

I can accept the fact that I no longer qualify for lap time, provided I get plenty of hand squeezes, back rubs, and hugs. If you can get enough of these, they're almost as good. During my loneliest hours, however, when I'm discouraged or grieving, I admit I'd like to turn back the clock and climb on my mother's lap, bury my head in her chest, and hear her heart beating. I'd like to listen to her rhythmic breathing and even enjoy the sounds of her stomach gurgling and growling. Being there never did make *all* the problems go away—it still wouldn't. But it would sure be wonderful. If I could be on her lap just once more, when I hopped down I'd have courage and strength to face the world again. I'd have a renewed belief in myself.

Are you ever too big to want your mom or your dad to hold you? Of course not! But please sit lightly, and do be careful. You wouldn't want to squish them flat, now would you?

4

Why Did God Make Zits and Other Disgusting Stuff?

I've got a zit on the end of my nose as I write this chapter. It's true. I wouldn't make up something like that. It's big, bright red, sore, and very embarrassing. I feel like His Royal Ugliness, and I feel that everybody who sees me is staring right at it. People down the block are probably gawking at my nose and making "Yuk" sounds. So are drivers in cars as they speed by. I'll bet even passengers in airplanes flying at forty thousand feet are revolted by my appearance. If I could, I'd hide in my room until it went away. I've thought of putting a giant bandage over it, but that would just attract more attention. When I go to the mall today, some little kid is going to think it's Christmas because I look exactly like Rudolph.

So tell me, why did God make humans with so many imperfections, especially on the parts of our bodies that show? God could have created us flawless, without a blemish or with fewer lumps and bumps than most of us have. At the very least, God should have put them in areas seen only by family members and those in the same P.E. class. The list of outward imperfections we humans must endure is staggering. If you have a weak stomach, maybe you better skip this next paragraph.

Here goes. There are birthmarks, cold sores, moles, cavities, chapped lips, warts, dandruff, split ends, freckles, athlete's foot, sleepers, boogers (oops, I meant to say nasal blockages), sties, boils, blackheads, ear wax, hangnails; and of course the number one problem, acne or pimples, also affectionately known as zits. I ask you, how can a loving God permit things such as these to afflict 99.9 percent of us?

Maybe at the beginning, when God sat in front of the drawing board, a choice had to be made between (1) designing perfect people, and (2) creating humans like us who make mistakes, leave messes behind, and get zits but who are free to make choices. Perhaps it's part of the grand scheme, a price we pay for being unique individuals, unrepeatable miracles who are able to think for ourselves. Still I'd like to know why, on the day of a major social event, my hair is always unruly, my eyes are bloodshot, or my face has millions of creases on it from sleeping tummy-side-down on a wrinkled sheet. I can go all year with an almost perfect complexion, and then the night before I'm supposed to give a report in front of a hundred people—*pow!*—out pops a humongous zit the size of Mt. Everest. Okay, so that's an exaggeration. It's more the size of Mt. Rushmore or perhaps the Washington Monument.

God certainly has a sense of humor. Have you looked at an aardvark, a hyena, a moose, or a wombat lately? It's possible that to keep humans properly humble, God threw in a few "flaws" in hopes we'd not take either them or ourselves too seriously, that maybe we'd even get a chuckle or two from our minor trials and tribulations. Actually, I seldom notice the outward imperfections on the people I love. I know how wonderful they are inside, and no exterior blemish makes a bit of difference.

Anyhow, even the most handsome and beautiful models in the world get runny noses, have smelly armpits, chew on their fingernails, have pieces of food stuck between their teeth, and get fuzz in their navels from time to time. Our common defects ought to make us compassionate toward one another since no one is completely immune from zit attacks.

Certainly, blemishes are clever little reminders from the Creator to take care of our physical body, which is, we're told in the Bible, "a temple of the Holy Spirit" (1 Corinthians 6:19). We can minimize some kinds of blemishes and other unpleasant conditions by getting adequate rest, eating a balanced diet, exercising regularly, and maintaining proper habits of hygiene. Zits in particular can be outward signs of inner changes, indications that our bodies are growing rapidly. They're a bother, but it may help to know they're the result of a very natural process.

The ultimate answer is to learn to accept ourselves as we are—warts, bumps, zits, and all. God does. And God knows a whole lot more about beauty than the biggest, fanciest mirrors ever have. God sees into our hearts and knows our motives. What counts is who we are on the inside. Zits are temporary. Love and goodness and peace are eternal. In theory, our outward appearance should have little to do with how we feel about ourselves. It doesn't always work quite that way; but remember: a good self-image is formed in our souls and is nurtured by positive thoughts, kind actions, and healthy relationships.

There is no doubt whatsoever that the worst blemishes in the world are not on people's skins but in their brains. Unloving attitudes are destructive and hurtful to entire groups, nations, and societies. The ugliest zits of all are greed, prejudice, violence, and hatred. There's no magic potion, no soothing ointment to apply to make them disappear. These defects go so deep they can be cured only by our becoming new people, by being reborn through the power of God's love. If you're looking for something to add to your prayer list, this might be it.

5

At My Age, Does It Matter What I Believe?

I t was 2:00 A.M. and Dad (that's me) was still up. So were three of our kids—teenagers Mike, Sara, and Dave. They needed to go to bed because they had school tomorrow. Actually, it was already tomorrow. I had to be to work by 7:30 A.M., and somehow manage not to yawn or close my eyes for the rest of the day. But what were the four of us to do? There was no way we could go to sleep in the middle of such a stimulating conversation. Our brains were in high gear as we discussed important theological issues over snacks and soft drinks. Our voices rose and fell according to how intensely we felt about a particular topic. Every so often, there was a quartet of speakers as we all talked at once. Mom, from the comfort of her warm bed, kept sleepily suggesting we tone it down.

We jumped from subject to subject, such as changes the church must make if it's to survive in the twenty-first century; the problem of evil and why so many bad things happen to good people; the reasons God does and doesn't answer our prayers. When we started arguing about which television evangelist has the most outrageous hairdo, we decided it must be time for bed.

I think I gained more in those three hours than I did in three years of systematic theology classes, though that might be a slight exaggeration. We debated, disputed, and occasionally even agreed on subjects. It wore us out, but it was a wonderful experience. We decided we couldn't stand to do something this exhausting very often—maybe only once or twice a year. Through the years, our conversations have continued. Come to think of it, we're about due for another session.

It is important for persons of all ages to think seriously about what they believe, to use their God-given minds to theologize—that is, to study and wrestle with who God is and what in the world God is doing. This certainly includes young people. It's crucial because our words and actions are based directly on what we affirm. If we believe in our hearts that God is love, we'll be able to see and respond to the love that's in other people. If we are convinced that God is forgiving, we'll be quicker to forgive our family and friends when they hurt us. If we really believe that Jesus wants us to serve others, we won't mind quite so much waiting at the end of the cafeteria line. We won't stay angry when somebody ignores us or lets us down.

During the preteen and early teen years, our beliefs usually aren't clearly formulated. In fact, we may feel wishy-washy about many of them. The solution is to keep working at it; to keep asking, wondering, and sharing. We may amaze ourselves by how profound and wise our thoughts really are. Anyway, who says we have to know everything? Nobody knows it all. The most scholarly students of the Bible and the oldest theology professors certainly don't know everything about the ways and will of God. Young people's opinions are every bit as valid and worthy of note as are those of adults who have accumulated many years of experience. It makes good sense, therefore, to pay attention to one another, especially to listen to the people we admire and trust.

Expect to feel strongly about some things and not so intensely about others. A few statements of faith will have bunches of exclamation points after them, like "I believe God wants us to live together in peace!!!" Or, "I know Jesus loves me a whole lot!!!" A long time ago these would have been called "pulpit pounders." They're beliefs you hold with conviction.

The majority of your beliefs may have plain old periods at the end of the sentences. These are explanations such as "I try to follow the Ten Commandments." Or, "God often speaks to me through music." Or, "I find God in the beauty of nature."

Still others will be followed by question marks. Don't worry if this is the case. It's normal and very healthy to have a bundle of questions. Quite likely you'll have as many questions about your faith when you're eighty as you do now, maybe even more.

Building and shaping your own individual theology—that is, developing a set of beliefs that works for you—is a lifetime endeavor. Hopefully you'll never finish growing in your faith; you'll always be adding fresh new understandings and leaving behind the worn-out ones. Try to learn and expand your mind every day of your life, from the cradle to the grave. Since God is continually up to new things and is forever creating, you and I had better be on our spiritual toes. When God asks us to change, we need to be flexible enough to respond at a moment's notice.

Personally, I doubt that I could write a book about my beliefs. It would be a jumble of incomplete ideas. I would have serious trouble just trying to compose a term paper on my beliefs, at least one that would make sense and earn a decent grade. I call what I have my "peanut butter and jelly" theology. I stammer a lot when I'm asked to explain it. My system of beliefs is pretty simple and basic—nothing fancy.

But it sure sticks to my ribs and nourishes my spirit. Plus, it's mine.

If you're ever in my neighborhood, stop by and let's compare theologies. I'll round up Mike, Sara, and Dave, make some hot chocolate, and pop a bag of popcorn in the microwave. But give me a couple of days' warning, please, so I can get caught up on my sleep first!

6

Please, God, Would You Reprogram My Brother?

Diary entries of a frustrated sister

ear Diary:
He's at it again. That little twerp is more of a bother than he is a brother. Saturday morning, my one day to sleep in, wouldn't you know it? He decides to dribble a basketball at 5:30 A.M. Naturally, his room is right above mine. I pounded on the ceiling with my tennis racquet, but do you think he quit? No way. So I stumbled up the stairs and ordered him to knock it off. You know what he said? "I don't have to 'cause you're only my sister. Anyway, I'm doing what Dad told me to do—practicing for the championship game next week."

"At 5:30 in the morning? I have half a mind to cram that ball down your scrawny throat!"

"I'll tell Mom." I took one teensy step toward him and he started yelling at the top of his lungs, "Mom! Mom! Angie's trying to hurt me!" If I'd been trying to do him bodily harm, which I wasn't, I'd have stuffed a pillow in his big mouth first. The boy's got a whiny voice the size of Texas. I went back to my room, pulled the covers over my head, and managed to get about twenty more minutes of sleep before the dog wanted to go outside. Plus the cat, who craves human companionship, decided to sit on top of my stomach.

Dear Diary:

He did it again. He claims it was somebody else, but I know better. He sneaked in my room and switched my shampoo for hand lotion. I'm so mad. In the shower I couldn't get the shampoo to foam at all. My hair just kept feeling greasier. I might never have figured out what he'd done, except when I made a dash to my dresser for another bottle of shampoo, he was standing in the hallway. "Having trouble getting your hair clean?" he asked. Then he made this evil-sounding snicker. I'd have run after him and snapped him with my towel, but I was already going to be late for school. He thinks he's so clever.

Dear Diary:

I used to have hopes that some day my brother would actually mature and become a decent human being. I've about given up. Before I was out of bed today he stretched clear plastic wrap over the top of the toilet. I didn't notice until it was too late. Hey, I was still groggy because I stayed up late last night finishing my English paper. At breakfast he was talking and eating cereal at the same time, and gobs of cereal and milk kept falling from his mouth. It grossed me out.

O God, if you are kind and loving, would you please reprogram my brother? That, of course, may be too big a job even for you. I'm not asking you to do anything drastic like getting rid of him, although if reprogramming doesn't work, that's not such a bad idea. I'd just like you to change some of his brain circuits or rearrange his hormones—something so I can stand to be in the same family with him. I will not be responsible for my actions if he doesn't straighten up soon.

Dear Diary:

Today he really did it. I mean he really, really did it! He read parts of my diary. I keep it locked, so he either found my key or picked the lock. Whichever, it doesn't much matter. He invaded my space and my privacy. I am not amused! Now he tells me he took notes and is going to blabber to Mom about some of the stuff he saw unless I give him all my desserts for the next six months. He's got to be the world's biggest jerk.

Dear Diary:

It's becoming increasingly apparent he's not going to change, at least not in the foreseeable future. As I calculate, I have two options: fight with him constantly or learn to put up with him; stay frustrated or become more patient. It has occurred to me that if I don't rise to his bait, he might stop casting his line in my direction. I'm sick and tired of his stunts. If I can act like they don't upset me, or better yet laugh at them, he'll probably decide his tricks aren't so much fun anymore. I'll try it, but I'm making no promises.

Dear Diary:

It's working, sort of. He used my favorite sweater to wipe the dust off the T.V. screen. I was just about to suffocate him with that sweater when I remembered my new approach. So I gave him a sisterly hug instead and said, "Thanks, bro, that makes the picture ten times clearer."

"You're not mad?" He seemed to be in shock.

"Nope, not a bit. My sweater was filthy and needed to go to the cleaners anyway. All you did was speed up the process. I should probably thank you for your help." He stood there speechless and bug-eyed with his mouth hanging open. It was my turn to snicker. My idea is paying off. Yippee!

Dear Diary:

He's becoming halfway human. He chewed with his mouth closed today, let me have the bathroom first, and held open a door for me. Miracles never cease.

Maybe you won't have to reprogram him after all, God, although a few minor adjustments may still be necessary. I've got my fingers crossed because I don't know how long this will last. A relapse could happen at any time.

I think I've learned a valuable lesson: that nagging never works for long. It's far better to nudge people gently into accepting new attitudes; to humor them into improving their behavior; to love them into changing irritating habits.

Dear Diary:

I'm thankful God made each individual free to become who she or he chooses to be. My little brother can still be a nuisance sometimes, but not like before.

So God, I no longer want you to mess with his head. He's pretty good just the way he is. By the way, the basketball tournament is over (his team lost) and he's on to soccer. He's taken all the drawers out of his dresser to use as a substitute goal. Fortunately a soccer ball is smaller than a basketball. I certainly hope he doesn't decide to take up hockey. You might hang on to my reprogramming request just in case. If he doesn't need it, there are a couple of his buddies I might like you to reprogram instead!

7

Why Can't I Talk to My Parents About Things That Really Matter?

The following is an open letter to parents. It's a compilation of thoughts and ideas shared by a wide variety of young people. They hope it contains helpful insights for families in stressful times like these.

Dear Moms and Dads of the World:

We know that communicating with us isn't always easy. We've been known to resist listening to you for no reason other than it's you speaking. Two minutes later somebody else may say the very same thing, and we'll immediately accept it as gospel. We mean no offense. That's just the way it is, and probably the way it was when you were our age.

Topics that matter the most to us, including our deepest feelings, are the hardest to share with you. When we try, we aren't always in close touch with our newly acquired emotions, or else we don't know quite the right words to express them clearly. After we've messed up, it's tough to say to you, "I'm sorry." When we've disappointed you, we have to gulp a few times before working up the courage to ask for a second chance. We may be young, but we have our pride.

Perhaps it's difficult to talk about important matters because we care a great deal what you think. We very much desire your approval and blessing. Perfect strangers are able to discuss controversial issues more readily than family members can. It's easier to unload your radical ideas on persons you'll never see again. It's different with family and close friends. You have to sit at the same dinner table with them, go to the same school, share the same bathroom, and see each other first thing in the morning.

Dear parents, we'd like to tell you more often how much we love you. For some reason the words usually come out wrong. We become tongue-tied. Our thoughts get twisted, and we end up saying something really dumb. Our hope is that you can read between the lines and understand what we mean. Of course, this can go both ways. Do you wish you could express your love for us more freely and frequently?

We admit we're quite accomplished at role playing. We outwardly act as though we're agreeing with you and willing to meet your expectations, when all the while our fingers are crossed. As soon as you're out of sight, we do what we intended to do in the first place. It might be plain old-fashioned stubbornness on our part; or it could be a significant step toward gaining our independence. We ourselves can't always tell which it is. So please be patient. We're doing the best we can.

You don't always seem to see us as real people. We're neither children nor adults, but we are "somebodies" who have genuine feelings, good ideas, and lots of promise. Sometimes you treat us as wind-up kids instead of maturing people with hopes and fears, with strengths and weaknesses. We're rapidly becoming capable of making our own decisions, of having good judgment, of effectively managing our own finances, and of following through on projects without being constantly reminded. In case you haven't noticed lately, we're no longer

Mommy and Daddy's little babies. It's been years since we needed you to cut the meat on our plate and wipe our noses.

Yes, we've been known to treat you with less than the respect you deserve. You're easy to take for granted. We may act as though you're stuck with us. You're required to provide for us and are supposed to be good to us because that's the way things are; it's the law.

Nevertheless, we want you to know we appreciate the job you're doing. We understand what a challenge it can be. Parenting is a twenty-four-hours-a-day, seven-days-a-week occupation. Once a parent, you're a parent forever. Isn't that kind of scary? We watch you worry about our progress in school, about your financial ability to help us in the future, and even about the kind of world you're sending us into. The anxiety shows on your faces and in the way your shoulders sag every so often. No wonder you occasionally get cranky. Come what may, we want you to know we love you and always will.

At times we question in our hearts how honest we dare to be with you. How much can we risk when we depend on you for our very existence? It's in our best interest to stay in your good graces, particularly if we need to ask a favor. We're not ready to face the world by ourselves. That's why we hem and haw when telling you a painful truth. Or we may offer it to you in small doses. We might be more blunt if we were confident you wouldn't be bent out of shape or threatened by it but were able to handle it gracefully.

Contrary to prevailing opinion, we really don't enjoy upsetting you. Apparently it's been a concern since the dawning of history that the messenger may sometimes be rejected along with an unpopular message he or she carries. It would help us truth-tell if we had assurances you'd consistently distinguish between who we are and what we say. You can reject the message if you wish. That's your privilege. But please continue to accept and love the messengers—in this case, us.

A major obstacle to talking about significant issues is finding the time, or should we say *making* the time? Both of us are super busy and constantly on the go. There are loud noises competing for our ears. And it's next to impossible to have a serious conversation when everybody's nearly exhausted, wiped out, or bone weary. Let's schedule some quality time. We know, we know, the earphones will have to come out. But don't get righteous on us. You get preoccupied, too. You go around with your heads crammed full of dates on the calendar, lists of duties, and your own private agendas which exclude us. We're willing to make adjustments for you and hope you'll do the same for us. When we sit down to have a conversation, we may sit on the couch and stare at each other for an hour in silence. But it's worth taking the chance. Who knows? Next time we may talk a blue streak into the wee hours.

We don't necessarily want answers when we ask questions, nor do we expect quick solutions when we share problems. We just want somebody to listen to us. We need parents who hear not only our words but our feelings as well. Sometimes adults give answers to questions we aren't even asking; and they're often long, drawn-out recitations that we find bor-r-ring. What we want is for you to give us a nod or a hug and say, "We understand." It would be refreshing when you didn't have an answer if you'd say, "I don't know, but let's find out together."

When it comes to offering irrelevant information, we think you adults are light-years ahead of us. You've had the benefit of experience. In addition, you can simply repeat the cliches your parents used on you. Do any of these following sayings sound familiar?

1. "Now when I was your age . . . blah, blah, blah." We'd like to know how somebody who can't remember where he or she put the car keys five minutes ago can remember what happened thirty years ago.

2. "If I've told you once I've told you (a) a hundred times, (b) a thousand times, (c) a million times." We suggest parents stop speaking in generalities and give the actual number, which is probably closer to single digits like two or seven.

3. "I wasn't born yesterday, you know?" Yes, we certainly do. You forget; we see you without your makeup on, when

you haven't shaved for three days, or when you've had a terrible day at work. Spare us the obvious!

4. "Because I say so, that's why!" You do have the authority to pull rank on us. Our advice, however, is that you save this pronouncement for the most important occasions. Overuse detracts from its effectiveness.

5. "This is for your own good." Right! An accurate translation is, "This is going to be painful or taste bad, and probably both."

We don't expect wise sayings to flow from your parental mouths every waking moment. We want honesty, even if the words come stammering out. Don't try to hide your mistakes from us. By seeing yours, we'll be helped in dealing with ours. That way we'll both learn.

We youth are just like everybody else. We pick up negative things quick as a flash. If you call attention to our irritating little habits, we'll notice yours. The only difference is we mention yours at our own risk and with the potential of having an unpleasant confrontation. If you complain about how messy our rooms are, we'll probably whine about how terrible dinner tastes. If you nag us about getting our homework done, we'll moan about how cheap you are when buying clothes. And so it goes. Pretty soon we're yelling and crying. It's a bummer for everybody. May we suggest meeting halfway with both sides promising to criticize less and praise more?

We hope our little discourse has been informative. This communication thing is a two-way street. Open, honest, sharing is one of the most precious gifts we can give one another. We happily pledge ourselves to the task of working at it.

Faithfully yours,
The Younger Generation

8

If Jesus Was Perfect, How Can He Understand a Klutz Like Me?

Confessions of an uncoordinated preteen

People can be really nice and yet be klutzes—like me, for instance. My friends seem to enjoy my company, but if there's a wall, some furniture, a car, or a bus within ten feet, I'll run smack dab into it. The bigger it is, the more likely I am to crash into it full speed ahead. I wear glasses, but that's not the problem. I guess I'm a world-class klutz. If there are stairs anywhere in a building, I'll find a way to fall down them. I'm so good at being a klutz I can fall *up* a flight of stairs. I've done it several times. I'm not exactly clumsy. In fact, I'm a member of our school's gymnastics team. But for some mysterious reason, I keep doing silly things. No major catastrophes, mind you; just minor mishaps. Some of my troubles are actually funny; some are downright hilarious. Even I have to laugh.

The other day I left the freezer door open a pinch. I didn't mean to. It looked like it was closed tightly. You'd have had to use a magnifying glass to see the crack. Twenty-four hours later you could sure tell it hadn't been completely closed. My dad went to get a dish of chocolate ice cream and came back with a bowl of icky brown soup. What a mess! My mom told me not to worry. The freezer was almost empty and was long overdue for defrosting.

I've done things like drop the butter dish upside down on our cat. I have to admit it was kind of exciting chasing a scared pet around the house trying to remove a blob of yellow goo from its back. I routinely burn my breakfast toast which sets off our smoke detector. Hey, my older brother should be out of bed anyhow. He's supposed to be in class by 8:00 A.M. I've gone entire days wearing a sweater wrong side out. How embarrassing to have that little tag in plain sight! I've worn socks that don't match and put my shoes on the wrong feet. Can you believe it?

When our family went to dinner the other night, I couldn't seem to make my mouth work right. I messed up my order big time. I did okay asking for the baked chicken, but I got everything else turned around. "I'd like pashed motatoes," I said. "No, make that a paked botato with cour scream." The waitress got the giggles and almost spilled a pitcher of water down my mom's back.

"Why don't you order French fries," my brother snickered. "You couldn't possibly goof that up, or *could* you?"

"Very funny," I said. I was getting flustered. "And the sean boup sounds good, too."

"I imagine you'll want some perry chie," chuckled our waitress. "Would you like cripped wheam on that?" I was starting to get mad. It seemed like everybody in the entire restaurant was cracking up. I would have gone home right then and there except I was starving. Well, hungry is a more accurate description. I have to admit I've never had to deal with starvation.

When I went to Sunday school that next Sunday, the lesson was about how Jesus was perfect. It got me to wondering. If

Jesus never did anything wrong and if he was completely perfect his whole life, how could he understand a big-time bungler like me? I probably made several dozen mistakes yesterday; and that was before lunch. Does God love klutzes like me? What if I'm doomed? I better ask our teacher, Mrs. McCormack, what she thinks. She's a smart lady. Wow! Am I glad I asked! We had a great discussion after class; then we had a telephone talk during the week. She said Jesus no doubt got blisters on his feet from walking on the rough, dusty roads of Galilee; that he may have had scars on his hands from working in his father's carpentry shop. Perhaps as a child he didn't like eating cooked vegetables. It could be that more than once he spilled his cup of goat's milk on the floor. We talked about how Jesus' motives were always pure, his words were always honest, and his actions always had integrity.

"Let me get this straight," I said. "Jesus was perfect inside, right? He was love and nothing but love. But maybe he didn't have a 4.0 GPA at the synagogue, maybe he built a chair with one leg too short, and maybe he overslept on a Sabbath and missed worship?"

"We don't know any of those things for certain," my teacher added, "but I think it's very possible. We believe that Jesus was sinless, not that he was a robot who never made any mistakes."

"That makes me feel a lot better. It means that Jesus understands me and doesn't reject me for all the crazy things I do. He might even get a good laugh over some of my shenanigans." I let out a big sigh and felt more relaxed than I had in months.

"We know for sure," continued Mrs. McCormack, "that Jesus' disciples were klutzes now and then. Sometimes they goofed up in critical situations, yet Jesus always loved them. I imagine he got frustrated with how slow they were to learn what he was trying to teach them. But Jesus was forgiving, patient, and kind. The Bible uses the phrase 'long-suffering.'

It means that God hangs in there with us. God never gives up on us, not ever."

I decided at that exact moment to start being more patient and kind with myself and to be more compassionate toward others. Who knows? This insight might even help me stop being such a klutz.

9

Do Zebras Have Black Stripes or White?

A parable about prejudice

My name is Steve, but my grandpa calls me Squirt. He's a great storyteller, a wonderful spinner of yarns and teller of tall tales. Even if I've got a hundred other things to do, when Gramps says, "Hey Squirt, have I got a doozy for you," I come running. I want to be comfortable because he sometimes gets lost trying to figure out how his stories will end. (By the way, Gramps is the only person in the world I let call me Squirt. I thought you ought to know.)

"Whatcha got for me today, Grandpa?" I asked, huffing and puffing from being out of breath.

"Well, it's sort of a parable about prejudice," he replied. I leaned back on the overstuffed chair, fluffed up the pillow, and got ready to listen. "Once upon a time," he began, "it seems there was a herd of zebras. Or is it a pride of zebras? No, that's lions. Maybe it's a gaggle."

"No, Gramps, a gaggle's a bunch of geese."

"You're right. I suppose it doesn't matter what a gathering of zebras is called. This group was a big, happy family. Everybody loved everybody else. They gladly shared their food

45

and helped one another find water. They took turns watching for predators like cheetahs and leopards. They were a picture of peace and tranquility as they grazed on the African savannah."

"So hurry up, Gramps, and get to the point. Tell me the good stuff; you know, when the trouble starts."

"Be patient, Squirt, I'm getting there. One bright and beautiful afternoon when the wind was perfectly still and the water was without a ripple, two old zebras came to the river to drink. Bending down, they saw their reflections in the pool.

" 'How is it,' asked the one, 'that my stripes are black and yours are white?' "

" 'Huh?' grunted the other. 'What do you mean? All these years I thought we looked exactly the same.'

" 'We're not alike at all. Take a closer look. You've got white stripes on a black background, and I've got black stripes on white.'

" 'You must have better eyes than I do. We look like identical twins to me.'

" 'Step back and squint really hard. Now what do you see?'

" 'Either a bunch of football referees or else two zebras going bonkers as they stare into a pool of water.'

" 'No, no, no. You see me with black stripes and you with white ones.'

" 'Even if I did, which I don't, what difference would that make? Aren't we both still zebras?'

" 'Yes, I suppose we are; but my appearance makes me much fancier, higher class, and far more important than you.'

" 'Just because you've got black stripes? No way!' When the two elders went back to the herd, they continued their argument. Pretty soon, the whole place was an uproar. Had a predator sneaked up on them at that moment, they'd have all been lunch; or at least a bedtime snack.

" 'We're every bit as good as you are,' snorted a white-striped zebra who nervously pawed the dirt, stirring up a cloud of dust. Meanwhile, the youngsters were playing and cavorting in the soft, gentle grass. 'What's all the ruckus?' asked a yearling.

" 'Oh, probably the same silly stuff as always. Those adults are having another one of their discussions.'

" 'But this time they sound angry. Everybody's jumping up and down and yelling. Let's go over and find out what the problem is.' Before they could so much as ask a question, zebra parents grabbed their children and hid them in the bushes.

" 'What's going on?' the young ones whispered.

" 'Those zebras over there have been asked to leave. They're no longer welcome. You'll never play again with any of their offspring. You see, they're inferior to us. They have white stripes.'

" 'They don't look any different to us. We don't want them to go. They're our best friends. Besides, how can you adults tell who has which color stripes?'

" 'Easy,' replied their elders. 'It's all in the tail. If the very tip has a black band, you're one of us. But if the tip is white, you're one of them.' The two groups of zebras moved farther apart, stomping their hooves and shouting at one another.

" 'But Mom, Dad, we don't want them to go away. We like the white-striped zebras. Who will we play with now?'

" 'Hush up. We're doing this for your own good.' Soon the black stripes were alone on the east part of the field where vegetation was lush and water plentiful. The white stripes were huddled on a patch of rocky ground far to the west."

Gramps paused, got up and went to the kitchen to make a cup of tea. I guess storytelling makes a person thirsty. I followed right behind him.

"Gramps," I pleaded, "you can't stop now. I like stories with happy endings."

"So do I, Squirt. So do I. Sometimes, though, it just doesn't turn out that way."

"But you're the one doing the telling. You can make it come out any way you want."

"I wish I could. I may exaggerate sometimes and use my imagination, but even experienced yarn-spinners like me finally have to tell the truth. Enough of this philosophizing. Let's get on with the story."

I decided to lean against Gramps. He put his big arm around me and continued.

"Years went by. The black-striped zebras prospered and grew plump while the white stripes struggled to maintain their meager existence."

"That's not fair, Gramps," I interrupted. "Can't you do something to fix it?" He slowly stroked his chin before answering.

"Well, maybe there is one thing I could do. You remember those young zebras who played together? It seems that one blistering hot day, when the black-striped youngsters were lying in the shade, a cheetah came speeding toward them through the bush. Meanwhile in the territory of the white stripes, a lion came skulking at them. In their haste to find safety, both groups ran into each other at the middle of the savannah. They found a place to hide, and when the danger was past, they stayed together and talked for a while.

" 'Hey, I know you. I used to play jump-the-mud-puddle with you. You're cute.'

" 'And you're handsome,' replied the other. Soon everybody was visiting and having a grand time. It wasn't long, however, before a few of the old folks got wind of it, scolded them, and sent the bunch of them home."

"What kind of happy ending is that, Gramps?" I complained.

"Best I can do on short notice, Squirt. But let me ask you a question. Do young people always do what their elders tell them?"

"Not always."

"Maybe zebra kids don't either." A few days later, it's entirely possible there were pint-sized zebras hopping around in the dry grass, having so much fun they didn't notice whose tail had what color tip; who didn't care one bit whether stripes were black on white, white on black, or purple on green."

"H-m-m-m. That's got possibilities," I said, feeling a little better.

"I'm glad, too," Gramps replied. "I wonder what new, positive endings you young folks may add to our human story."

10

How Can I Ever Learn Enough to Meet Tomorrow's Challenges?

The teacher finished taking roll and opened her Bible. "Today's lesson is 'How can I ever learn enough to meet tomorrow's challenges?' It's a tough question, but the answer is in this book." She tapped her finger on the Bible. "Don't groan. I promise this will be interesting. It's from Numbers, the fourth book in the Old Testament. I know, I know—it happened over thirty-two hundred years ago. But just because something took place in days of yore doesn't mean it's boring and of no value. This is great stuff!

"Moses sent spies into the land of Canaan, into the Promised Land to scope the place out—you know, to see how tough the folks who already lived there were and to check on the food supply and the economic potential of the territory. Forty days later they came back and said, 'We've got some good news and some bad news. First of all, it's a land flowing with milk and honey.' They sounded like real estate salespeople making their pitch: 'There are zillions of grapes and tons of wheat, not to mention nuts and figs and barley. Sure, the Promised Land needs some work, but it's got possibilities.'

" 'Let's pack up and get going!' shouted the people, who had become tired of wandering through the wilderness for forty years.

" 'Not so fast,' the spies replied. 'You haven't heard the bad news yet. There's this minor problem. The residents are huge—they're giants. They're big enough to be professional wrestlers or defensive linemen for the Chicago Bears.' Okay, that's not quite what they said, but it's a close approximation. Anyway, they informed the Hebrew people that 'when these monsters walk, the ground shakes beneath their feet. Then when we looked in a mirror, we seemed pretty puny by comparison, kind of like grasshoppers. It's obviously too big a job for small folks like us. We could get hurt, squished like bugs. It's overwhelming. The risks are too great. Let's go back to Egypt.'

"I know how those spies felt, and I'll bet you do, too. Many of us have the same overwhelmed feelings when we look at the work that lies ahead of us and our world. There's simply too much to learn, too many world problems to fix, too many major decisions to make. The challenges are enormous, and we're pretty small. How can we ever learn enough about history to keep from repeating the same old mistakes? Even if we stay in school for the rest of our earthly lives, we can never learn enough about electronics, computers, physics, mathematics, economics, the arts, communications, biology, agronomy, medicine, international affairs, and on and on. Our brains are marvelous creations, but they do have their limits. In the face of all these demands, is it any wonder we appear to be runts or scrawny little grasshoppers? When lined up against societal problems, we look like a middle-school football team opposing the San Francisco Forty-Niners."

How I remember being scared at the beginning of every school year, especially when I was entering a new school. Would people like me? Would I make any friends? Could I keep pace academically with more difficult and complex subjects? I was a bundle of "what-ifs." What if I flunk out? What if nobody will eat lunch with me? What if I can't get my locker opened? What if my teachers are mean and cranky? I felt buried under all the requirements those first few days of class. There were daily assignments, book reports, pop quizzes, term papers, and final exams. There were expectations like class participation and regular attendance; and worst of all for a person as painfully shy as I am, oral reports. I dreaded having to do that. Weeks in advance my stomach got nervous. But I survived. I made it. And I have several framed documents on my office wall to prove it!

Maybe we can't learn everything, but so what? More important than knowing an impressive amount of information is acquiring the intellectual tools to figure things out yourself, possessing the mental and spiritual disciplines necessary for growth, and knowing where to go for help when all else fails. Hang in there with me while I offer a few insights into how to accomplish all this. It's not just a neat trick. It's a partial list of techniques for surviving in the twenty-first century.

1. Be a good listener. Pay attention to the words and wisdom of others and not just of those who look, act, and think like you do. We need not only to keep our eyes open but also to be open people who accept others and are receptive to new methods, ideas, and ways. The individuals I admire most never stop learning and give honest hearings to even the most controversial concepts.

2. Strive to be positive, creative, and inventive. A wrong idea isn't the end of the world, but a negative attitude might well be. It's doesn't matter if you mess up a thousand times when you learn in the process. As a result of that struggle, you may get it right on try number 1,001. It takes a heap of strength to keep plugging and lots of courage to be innovative. It requires special people to go where few humans have ever gone before.

3. Plan for all you're worth, but when you start working on the plan, take one step at a time. Even baby steps will eventually get you to your destination. Remember: Rome wasn't

built in a day, and neither were the ideas inside your brain or the wisdom within your soul. All the knowledge you'll need for your life's journey cannot be crammed in at once. Be patient. As you proceed, there'll be a special nook or cranny for each thought.

4. Make certain you're heading the right direction, which will always move you toward helping others. Trying to become smarter simply to be smarter or to impress people just doesn't cut it. The purest motives and highest goals of learning are to love people and to serve humanity.

5. Find a calm, peaceful center within yourself. When things start to get out of hand and the pressures are great, seek a place of inner quietness. Dwell there for as long as it takes to calm your soul. Then take a deep breath and head back to the fray. You'll be focused and energized. Whatever the tasks or problems, they won't seem quite so overwhelming anymore.

Now then, here comes the important, heavy-duty stuff. It's not how much or what you know that counts. It's who you are. You could be a whiz kid, the cleverest person on the entire continent. But if you aren't kind and loving, so what? Your mind and heart need to work in concert and to communicate with each other. Your head may think, "I know a whole lot. I've got connections and all kinds of answers." But your heart should also speak up with a suggestion like, "That's cool. Now get out there and use that brain power to help somebody." Maybe you've memorized the names of state capitals in Montana and Maine. That's fine and dandy. But what if you never notice that the elderly woman at the end of your block needs her lawn mowed or her leaves raked? You may pass your next American history test with flying colors but flunk the most important lessons of life.

Ten or fifteen years from now you may have impressive letters after your name such as B.A., M.S., R.N., C.P.A., or the like. If you do, you'll have reason to be proud. You'll have accomplished something very significant. But maybe we ought to define these initials in new and different ways. What if M.D. didn't only stand for Doctor of Medicine but also meant

"Doer of Mercy"? And what if B.S. referred both to the Bachelor of Science degree and also to having a "Beautiful Spirit"? Ph.D. actually means Doctor of Philosophy, but why couldn't if be "Provider of Hopes and Dreams" as well?

So that's it. Please remember how those folks thirty-two hundred years ago put one sandal in front of the other and crossed over into the Promised Land. The rest, as they say, is history. Now it's our turn. Let's go for it!

11

Can I Cram for God's Final Exam?

A conversation between two friends

Whatchadoin'?"

"Studying for God's final exam."

"Oh, sure."

"No, really. I read the Bible every day, faithfully go to Sunday school, actually pay attention to our preacher's sermons, and pray each night before I go to bed and in the morning when I get up."

"Hey, I'm impressed. But how do you know what the questions are going to be? Or for that matter, how do you know God gives a final exam at all?"

"I don't, not for sure. But just in case, I want to be ready. I figure if I study God's Word, the Bible, I'll cover the necessary material. I've been highlighting neat passages and taking notes."

"You're really serious about this, aren't you?"

"Yes, I am."

"Well, personally I am not going to cram, 'cause I'm not planning on appearing before the throne of judgment, or whatever it's called, for a long, long time. I'm only eleven. I'm going to wait to cram until I'm eighty or ninety, minimum."

"Suit yourself. Of course, nobody knows what may happen tomorrow, or even later today. My dad says it's better to be safe than sorry. He says stuff like that at least once a day and twice a day on weekends. I guess he wants to make certain I get the message."

"Don't laugh, but I've been doing some serious thinking of my own. I've got a few heavy-duty brain cells, too. Anyway, I don't believe God's going to make us pass a test before letting us into heaven. You think taking a semester test in math or history is pressure? All that's at stake there is a dumb old grade or maybe having to listen to your parents lecture you on the virtues of hard work. Just wait until you're sitting at a desk outside the pearly gates with a No. 2 pencil in your sweaty little hand, and your eternal destination hangs in the balance. You better have several spare pencils that are sharpened plus a good eraser. Does the Book mention whether God penalizes you for guessing?"

"It won't be like that at all. In my imagination I see God behind a huge oak desk and me sitting on the edge of a big chair. God's got a report card with the details of my entire life on it. I think the final exam will be like a divine interview, kind of cozy and friendly."

"Hm-m-m-m. That's an interesting thought. It makes a lot more sense than a true-false or multiple-choice quiz. But I'm still not ready to accept that a loving God would put us in a pressure cooker like this. It's scary just thinking about it. Some people, me for instance, don't do well on tests. I panic and go into a deep freeze. Maybe it's a wild idea, but suppose it's not God who makes the decision about eternal life but us?"

"People like you and me? No."

"Yes."

"God would never go for it. If folks have any smarts at all, they'd pick heaven. Nobody would ever choose that other place. And what about the idea that God divides the sheep from the goats? Of course being a city kid, I've never figured out what makes sheep so great or what those poor goats did to deserve such a fate."

"Me neither. What I'm trying to say is, maybe it's all based on the way we live—you know, how much we love each other, the helpful deeds we do, and the goodness in our hearts."

"That worries me almost as much as having to take a final exam. Have you seen my room? It's a disaster. I can also be the world's worst grouch; I procrastinate like the dickens; and I've been known to have a smart aleck mouth with adults."

"Come on, that's not what I mean. God isn't the 'Great Accountant' or someone with little nose glasses holding a thick ledger. God feels what we feel, understands our motives, knows the problems we face, and gives us the benefit of the doubt. At least I hope that's how it works."

"Sounds okay to me. In other words, if there is a final exam, which may or may not be the case, God won't ask questions about the insignificant, picky things that bend us humans out of shape."

"Exactly! Like dust-mopping under my bed or cleaning behind the refrigerator."

"Or forgetting to floss for two days. Or cutting out an article before anybody else has had a chance to read the newspaper."

"Or talking on the phone for an hour and a half."

"Or being five minutes late for class."

"Right. Some people believe God will allow only a certain number of souls into heaven. They say there's a divine quota or something. When it's full, I guess St. Peter would turn on the flashing 'No Vacancy' sign."

"You're joking."

"Yeah, I am. But do you think that's the way it really is? Does God grade on the curve? If so, for every 'A' God hands out, there'd be an equal number of flunks."

"That would be a bummer. I believe each person on earth has an equal chance and that God really wants everybody to have eternal happiness."

"Me, too. You know what just popped into my brain? No? Okay, I'll tell you. People who stew and fret all the time about what happens in the next life may miss the joy and beauty of this life."

"I get it. It's like when we take the church van to a youth rally. Getting there is half the fun. I love visiting, singing, and laughing together. Reaching the destination is important, but so is making the journey."

"We're on to something here. I think God gets a kick out of being our constant companion as we struggle along day by day. God would miss us a lot if we waited until the very end of our lives, then suddenly showed up and said, "Okay, I'm ready to be your friend.' "

"Good point. By the way, what time does your Bible study group meet?"

"Tomorrow at 8:00 A.M. How come you're asking?"

"Because I plan to attend. I have one question, though. Are there any tests? My knowledge of the Bible is pretty rusty, and it wasn't so great to start with."

"Nope, no tests. You can leave your No. 2 pencil at home, unless you plan to take notes."

"See you in the morning."

"Super. Want me to give you a wake-up call?"

12

Are There Any Heroines or Heroes Left?

Daniel's courage in the lion's den, Samson's physical strength, Ruth's love and faithfulness, Deborah's ability to judge, David's leadership and poetic skill, Martha's service and Mary's spirituality, Paul's missionary zeal—these are but a few of the virtues of heroines and heroes whose deeds are recorded in the Bible. A complete listing of important biblical characters and their exploits would fill the pages of this book.

The people we admire today often behave quite differently from these biblical personalities. We look up to the most famous people in our society, to those with the most political clout and economic power, to the richest and most beautiful. We give status to those whose pictures appear most frequently in magazines and newspapers, who are visible on television and in movies, whose voices are heard on records, tapes, and CDs. We tend to idolize professional athletes, rock stars, show business personalities, and wealthy business owners. In other words, our modern definitions of hero and heroine have changed dramatically from those of centuries past.

Occasionally a person on the contemporary scene who is a

servant of humanity becomes a hero or heroine—Pope John Paul II, Mikhail Gorbachev, Martin Luther King, Jr., and Mother Teresa. Sadly, the list historically has had far more male than female names. Thankfully this is changing, although we need to do our part to make certain change continues.

Heroines and heroes are almost always older than their fans. There are solid reasons for this fact. The older a person is, the greater her or his experience, the more time a person obviously has had to accomplish things, and the more opportunities there've been to learn about life. Yet several of my own role models are younger than I; some are "mere" youth. Paul understood this possibility when he advised the young Timothy, "Let no one despise your youth, but set the believers an example in speech and conduct, in love, in faith, in purity" (1 Timothy 4:12).

One young adult is my hero for international affairs. He's been an exchange student twice, is fluent in several languages besides English, and shares with me a vision of what the world could be if there were unity and harmony. He has challenged me to think globally, to work and pray for peace, and to see all people as my equals—as my sisters and brothers. I wouldn't be surprised if some day he becomes the U.S. Secretary of State. I don't have to wait, however, until a person becomes outwardly important before she or he can have a significant influence on my life. Though I'm nearly three times this young man's age, he's still my hero.

Then there's a teenager who's my heroine of caring for the earth. Most of us older folks didn't grow up with an awareness of the need to protect the environment. We took for granted that everything would remain clean and beautiful, that there'd always be plenty of pure water and fresh air. Were we ever mistaken! This young woman raised my consciousness about environmental issues from major problems like the depletion of the ozone layer and the loss of old-growth forests, to daily habits like using both sides of a three-by-five-inch note card, not leaving the faucet on the whole time I brush my teeth, and recycling even a few aluminum cans, cardboard boxes, or glass bottles.

I have tremendous admiration for young people who are disciplined in academic studies, who are musically gifted, or who are committed to athletic endeavors. I find it very inspiring to attend a school concert or a sports event. I am continually amazed at the high level of dedication these students bring to their activities. This is faith in action.

Several years ago the members of a youth group became my heroes and heroines. They wanted to make a difference in their community and decided to raise funds to help alleviate world hunger. A lengthy and animated discussion followed about various moneymaking projects. None of the traditional methods—car washes, bake sales, or doing yard work—seemed to appeal to anyone. "Why don't we have a marathon of some kind?" suggested Kathy. "You know, get pledges for walking ten kilometers or bowling three games."

"That's a great idea!" said Jim, one of their adult leaders. "How about doing something people your age find very difficult?"

"What's that?" the group asked.

"Being quiet."

"We could do it if we wanted to. How long would we have to be silent?" They debated among themselves about the wisdom of such a project.

"Could you be silent for twenty-four hours?" asked Jim.

"You bet!" they said at first. "Well, we *think* we could. Maybe. After all, a whole day is a long time. Could we make a little bit of noise, maybe whisper, or listen to music if we use earphones?"

"Nope. Let's go for total silence."

"What shall we call our idea?"

"I know," said Kathy. "We can call it a 'Quiet-A-Thon.' "

The twelve kids of the youth group set out to get pledges. People chuckled as they thought about twelve preteens being quiet for one complete day.

"I'll double my gift if you can pull this off," offered a number of people. The big day arrived. The youth group brought their sleeping bags, snacks, and reading material. They studied their Bibles, did homework, played games, worked crossword puzzles, prayed, and caught up on their sleep. They had a wonderful time together, though I don't think so much as one word was spoken that entire twenty-four hours. Best of all, that small group earned over seven thousand dollars to give to a local food bank and to contribute to their church's mission fund. One individual was so impressed with their effort, she donated a thousand dollars.

Maybe it's time to redefine what we mean by these two familiar words—*hero* and *heroine*. We need to let go of our pre-occupation with fame and fortune and focus instead on admiring people who are whole, emotionally healthy, loving, and compassionate. Our heroine or hero might be a teacher who is devoted to her or his students and works eighty hours a week not because of the salary but for the satisfaction of helping others learn and mature. Our hero or heroine could be a secretary who quietly and without credit holds an organization together and who fills in for others when they're sick or absent and doesn't expect so much as a "thank you." These heroines and heroes are servant people, not highly paid, socially correct, or important by any outward measures. Yet the rest of us cannot get along without them. They are humble but essential parts of society.

Using this more Christ-like definition, each and every one of us has the potential to grow into heroic stature. With God's help, you and I can become heroines and heroes! Goodness knows our world needs us!

13

Do I Doodle, Dawdle, and Dream Too Much?

young person asked a wise teacher this question: "Do I doodle, dawdle, and dream too much? I hope not, because they're the joys of my life."

"And why," replied the sage, "do you ask this question?"

"Because people say I do. They tell me I lack concentration. They say things like 'Keep your nose to the grindstone.' Personally, I think that would be rather painful."

"Me, too. Well, let's start with doodling. How frequently do you engage in this particular activity?"

"Every time I talk on the telephone. I make this neat doodle art with circles and squares and cute little triangles. My geometry paper never looked so cool. Or when I think really hard, like when I'm studying for a test, I draw weird squiggles and make strange designs. You ought to see the far-out cartoons I make on Sunday bulletins during the worship service."

"Bring them by sometime. I'd enjoy that. Who knows, maybe Rembrandt or Van Gogh started off the same way. Doodling can be a good way to relax and express your creative energy. I wonder how many of the world's great inventions began as absent-minded scribbling on scraps of paper. As long as you don't write on important documents or deface public places with graffiti, doodling is a healthy pastime. One of these days we'll have to do some group doodling and play ticktacktoe. Of course I get the *X* first."

"Okay, but what about dawdling? I stick around after school and talk to my friends and sometimes to teachers; or I sit in the library until it closes, and they finally chase me out. Then I'm late arriving home so I get in trouble. But I don't think I've done anything wrong."

The wise one answered, "Indeed you haven't. However, when you know you're going to be late, it's thoughtful to give somebody a call. That way they won't worry so much."

"Agreed. For some reason the time I dawdle most is Saturday. I spend the entire morning holed up in my room."

"Doing what?" inquired the teacher.

"Making journal entries, listening to music, writing poetry, stuff like that."

"Wonderful! Let me ask you another question. Do you manage to get your work done on time?"

"Usually. I'm actually rather prompt, but I don't always do things when other people think I should. That's what gets me into trouble."

"I assume you're talking about school assignments and chores around the house, things of that nature?"

"Exactly."

"You will have to learn to meet those expectations. There'll be deadlines like that for the rest of your life. But don't let that make you give up dawdling. Just make sure dawdling never interferes with your other responsibilities. Dawdling is getting to be a lost art, you know, in our hurried and harried society. I'll bet a lot of discoveries in art and science resulted from someone's dawdling. Isaac Newton, for example, had to sit under that apple tree long enough for an apple to fall off and clobber him on the noggin!"

"I suppose dawdling in the bathroom is another matter?"

"Probably," said the teacher. "It falls under the category of being considerate. Let me remind you, though, that taking time for oneself is very important. We all need to meditate, reflect, and remember. Don't let people call you lazy when what you're really doing is contemplating, praying, or thinking about the future. All persons need the space to expand their inner lives, to think, and to grow."

"Thanks. I guess I'm a quiet individual by nature. I seem to require lots of 'me' moments."

"So do I. Have you ever noticed that music has rests? The reason is to allow notes to breathe, to have freedom to move about, and to express themselves. Art needs empty spaces for there to be focus and definition. Relationships need occasional silence to permit the communication of deep, unspoken truths. Our problem these days," continued the teacher, "isn't too much dawdling, it's too *little* dawdling. We're constantly busy and seriously over-programmed. We let ourselves be rushed and crowded every hour of the day and night. Cherish all the dawdling you can manage to squeeze out of your hectic schedule."

"Thank you. I will. As a matter of fact, I'm heading to my favorite place of meditation right now."

"Oh," said the wise one, "is that under the leafy canopy of a massive tree, or perhaps in a chapel with stained-glass windows?"

"No, the bathtub. I have some of my best conversations with God while I'm soaking in hot water and surrounded by bubbles."

"I think this brings us to your third item," offered the teacher, "*dreaming.* Do you realize that God began everything with a dream, that the universe was once a glorious vision? Then God put words with the dream and spoke them out loud. 'Let there be light. Let there be water and sky and earth. Let there be vegetation and animals. Let there be human life.' And it was so. But first was the dream in the mind of God. Since you are made in God's image, that's how creativity works for you as well."

"I've never thought of it quite that way. I'm feeling much better. Thank you."

"You're welcome. It should be obvious that our world needs to encourage its poets, wise persons, visionaries, prophets, artists, composers, and spiritual leaders—in other words, its doodlers, dawdlers, and dreamers. Yes, faithfully fulfill your obligations; do your work. But also dream. Unleash your brain. Go on adventures inside your head. Explore ideas; play with words; chase after thoughts. After you have a plentiful supply, put them in a pouch and be a Johnny Appleseed of dreams, scattering them to the wind."

"I'd love to! While I'm at it, I think I'll fulfill a few other fantasies and swish through autumn leaves, walk barefoot in wet grass, dance in the moonlight, and blow dandelion seeds into the air."

Then the great teacher asked the young person the same question: "Can a person doodle, dawdle, or dream too much?"

"Never!" the youth shouted. And the two of them went off hand in hand to a nearby pond to skip round, smooth rocks.

14

Why Is It So Hard to Forgive Myself?

About a week ago I had one of those "anything times zero" days. The harder I tried, the more I goofed up. Every time I turned around, something else went wrong. I really got upset with myself. Regardless of my efforts, the results came up empty. I accomplished nothing, zip, zilch. It was like when you multiply a number times zero. The product will be zero, always and forever. It doesn't matter how big the other number is. Make it a million billion to the trillionth power if you wish. As soon as you multiply that by zero, you're instantly back to the beginning. Your sheet of paper that moments ago was covered with numbers is now blank and resembles a herd of sheep in a blinding snowstorm—solid white.

It was a glorious day to be alive, or so I'm told. The sun rose in brilliance and glory, but I never noticed. I was too busy grumping around the house because I couldn't get a turn in the bathroom. We were out of milk, so I couldn't eat my favorite cereal. Grumpiness piled up deeper and deeper. I left a trail of it wherever I went. Work turned out to be one disaster after another. Everything I touched ended up giant goose eggs. I felt like pouting in a corner somewhere and sucking my thumb. Given the rotten mood I was in, I would have missed the most wonderful blessing in the universe even if God had plopped it right in front of me.

Fortunately, this attitude was short-lived. By the next day I was my usual happy-go-lucky, fun-to-be-with person. Well, at least people could stand to be with me! As I reflected on my previous downer of a day, I realized my main problem was an unforgiving attitude. I spend my waking hours holding grudges against others, and most damaging of all, I was ticked off at myself. I couldn't seem to forgive myself for having negative feelings and behaving stupidly. I discovered once again that sometimes the hardest person in the world to forgive is yourself.

I can be very tough on myself. I can be very sweet and pleasant to others but act like a colossal grouch to myself. I mutter and mumble a lot and use some very unflattering names for myself when I get upset. "Weirdo" is about the nicest one. It's better if I keep the others out of print. Maybe it's hard to forgive myself because I know so much about me. I'm aware of every little mistake I make, every sneaky thing I do, every cross word and cuss word I say. Perhaps my expectations for myself are unrealistic. My head tells me I don't have to *be* the best although I should try to *do* my best. But my insides send a different message. "Got to be perfect, got to be perfect," they keep whispering. Well, only one person on this planet ever managed that, and his name was Jesus.

I really do like myself. I have a rather good self-image. But every so often I get on my own nerves. I do the same dumb things over and over again. You'd think I'd learn. It's downright discouraging. I wonder if I'm too concerned about my reputation, about what my peers think of me. Will they like me if I'm totally honest about how I feel and what I believe? The opinion of others isn't even in the same ballpark compared to how I feel about myself. If I have to choose between being liked by others and being honest with myself, there's no choice at all. I come first. That doesn't mean I'm self-centered or selfish. I'm the one who has to live with me for the rest of my life. Anyway, if my friends can't accept me when I'm truthful, then maybe they weren't such great friends in the first place. Perhaps I ought to set an example of how you can maintain personal integrity and still be popular, although no doubt it's easier said than done.

When you fail to be forgiving toward yourself, the results are never positive. You end up with inner turmoil and anger. Believe me, being bitter is a bummer. It brings your growth as a person to a screeching halt. Thank goodness, there's another possibility. We can accept God's gift of forgiveness, which has marvelous healing properties. There is nothing anyone can do, no thought or action so terrible, that it will place them outside the bounds of forgiveness. Forgiving yourself means you're free to move on in your life, ready to start over as a fresh, new person, and able to celebrate life and to live joyfully.

Forgiving ourselves and others is not a one-time event. It's an ongoing process, a way of living. It's a spiritual discipline you can learn and improve with practice. Since we humans continue to hurt others and harm ourselves, forgiveness needs to be continuous, too. It's a necessary part of unconditional love. But don't confuse forgiveness with an "anything goes" attitude. It doesn't mean I can go out and do as many rotten things as I want, saying "What's the difference? It doesn't matter who I hurt or the trouble I cause. I can always be forgiven again." True, there is no limit to the number of times God will forgive us. But the consequences of that wrongful behavior are lasting. When a person knows deep down that she or he is truly forgiven, there's a renewed desire to be compassionate, kind, considerate, and loving. In a phrase, forgiveness allows us to "let go and let grow."

How can you tell when you're a forgiven and forgiving person? You'll experience yourself like the earth immediately after a sudden summer rainstorm, all bright and sparkling with a pure, sweet odor. You won't see the problems in people— you'll see their potential and focus on their strengths and abilities. You'll hardly even notice their irritating habits and limitations. Your thoughts and attitudes will feel as if they stepped out of the shower, squeaky clean, invigorated, and refreshed. You'll feel as if you just took that first bite of a double-decker ice cream cone on a blistering hot afternoon, or as if you smelled a fragrant rose.

When I fail to let God forgive me, a strange thing happens. I lose my whistle. Oh, I'm not even very good at whistling in the first place. I can't reach the high notes, and the low ones are usually off-key. But I enjoy it. I don't whistle for the benefit of others. I do it for me. When I'm feeling good inside, my lips just naturally pucker up and let loose with a tune. But when I'm holding on to bitterness, mad at someone, or generally in a foul and unforgiving mood, I can't whistle. All that comes out of my mouth is a hissing sound—no music, just my breath exhaling rapidly. That's one measure of how I know whether I'm in a forgiving mood.

It would be a good time right now to go with me for fries and a soft drink. I'd be pleasant company, plus I'd probably pay the bill and leave a tip, too. How do I know? I'm whistling the old gospel hymn "Amazing Grace."

15

What If There's No Answer in the Bible?

Okay, it's quiz time. Let's play a little Bible trivia. I have five questions for you. If you get any right without looking them up, you will receive an automatic A + with a gold star thrown in as an additional reward.

1. Give the name of the son of Jonathan and grandson of Saul that begins with the letter *M*.

2. How long were Noah, his family, and all those animals cooped up in the ark before the rains came and the floods began to rise?

3. The Letter to Philemon is tucked between which two other New Testament epistles?

4. What delicacies tickled the palate of John the Baptist while he was in the desert?

5. What is the correct sequence of these three words spoken by Jesus in Matthew 7:7?

    a. seek, knock, and ask

    b. ask, knock, and seek

    c. seek, ask, and knock

    d. ask, seek, and knock

  e. knock, ask, and seek

  f. none of the above

If you're wondering what these questions have to do with anything, you're a jump ahead of me. Truly knowing the Bible is not a matter of remembering disconnected bits of information. It's far more than that. It's being aware of the major biblical themes; having a grasp of significant people, places, and events; understanding how God has worked in and through those events; coming to appreciate, even to love the Word of God contained in each of the sixty-six books in the Bible.

People of every age complain sometimes that the Bible doesn't have concise answers to many of today's problems. For example, you can find justification for both sides on the issue of capital punishment. And biblical writers couldn't address questions such as the use of nuclear energy and gun control. You'll find no references in its pages to AIDS, cancer, or heart disease; on eating disorders or the depletion of fossil fuels. It offers no *specific* guidance when dealing with the controversial subject of abortion.

Shall we simply throw out the Bible and junk it for more contemporary, up-to-date resources? By no means! It's far and away the most useful, precious guide to life that Christian people have. If, however, you're looking for easy, snap-your-fingers solutions to complex issues, you'll be very disappointed. The Bible was created by a wide variety of inspired persons over a period of more than a thousand years. Disciplined study is required in order to uncover the great biblical truths and principles. If you want simplistic answers, go buy a "How-to" paperback. The Bible offers something far more valuable than telling readers what to wear, when to blow their noses, or what to have for dinner. It contains general principles for living an abundant life; it serves as a spiritual map for our individual journeys of faith; it provides direction for the church; it shares words of hope for the world.

The Bible does have answers, many of them very practical and down to earth. It's just that to find them you must roll up your sleeves and start digging. There are abiding principles in its pages, from accepting unconditional love to having faith and trust, from living in peace and seeking justice to being thankful people, to knowing that we have received grace upon grace. We discover general rules of conduct and behavior for persons and for groups. The New Testament itself is nothing less than a radically new paradigm or pattern for living.

What do we gain if we know the proper order of seek, ask, and knock but do not know how to love? And of far greater value than knowing where Philemon is located is the knowledge that this epistle is a warm, personal letter asking a favor; that it gives us a glimpse into first-century life. The Bible contains a wealth of answers, but not of the simplistic variety.

Studying the Bible is similar to learning to spell correctly. The most helpful approach isn't necessarily to memorize every word. There are too many words in any language for most of us to accomplish that. But if we learn the basic rules of spelling and develop skill with phonetics, we'll be able to proceed in spelling with confidence. Just as rules give guidance to the speller, so also the Bible gives wisdom to those who seek.

Another example is mathematics. In geometry, once you've learned the basic theorems and postulates, you can use this knowledge to solve all kinds of complicated problems. Even though it's been decades since I took a math class, I still recall the rules for dividing fractions. I probably remember because they got pounded into my brain. After a million or so repetitions, it finally and permanently penetrated my skull. "When dividing fractions, invert the divisor and multiply." I hope you're impressed. Hey, it's been a lot of years!

When we open our Bible, the answers do not simply fall into our laps. God wisely arranged it so we'd have to cooperate. God expects us to use our minds, apply lots of good common sense, and study together. We shall be disappointed when we ask for neat, tidy answers in twenty-five words or less. Why do you think Jesus so frequently taught by using parables, by telling stories containing a variety of meanings? We hear about lost coins, about seeds planted in different soils, leaven in bread dough, and the fate of a roadside mugging victim. Jesus told homey tales because he wanted to engage the listeners' minds, make people draw their own conclusions, and encourage them to think for themselves.

Now then, you're probably wondering what the answers are to the Bible trivia quiz at the beginning of this chapter. I shall no longer leave you in suspense.

1. Jonathan's son was Mephibosheth (say Meh-fib'-o-sheth'), whose life was as difficult as his name is to pronounce.

2. Mr. and Mrs. Noah, their family, and the animals were shut in the ark for seven days before the floods came, probably the longest week they ever spent.

3. The brief letter of Paul to Philemon is nestled between the epistles to Titus and Hebrews. I don't really care if you retain this bit of knowledge. But do remember that this letter indicates how much the apostle Paul cared for people.

4. John the Baptist feasted on such gourmet treats as locusts (large grasshoppers) dipped in wild honey. No wonder his message was hard for people to swallow. You'd be cranky, too, from eating a diet of what was apparently the first fast food in recorded history.

5. The answer is (d): ask, seek, knock. But who cares in what order you list them? What counts is whether you understand their meaning and follow their instructions.

You have my permission to use these five questions to impress your friends with your biblical scholarship. However, don't be a smart mouth. Quoting scripture and knowing biblical facts are no big deals. Write the Words of God on your heart—now that's something worth celebrating!

As we get further and further away from biblical times, we shall no doubt encounter more and more questions that aren't expressly answered in its pages. Do not worry. The content of the Bible is timeless. It's a book for every historical period and for every culture. It shall surely stand the test of time. God's Word will abide for eternity.

16

Why Can't I Always Be Happy?

No matter what your mood, there's a song to fit it. You say you're feeling joyful and happy? Try some Christian rock. That ought to keep your spirits bright. But you don't do well on a test the next day, and your best friend lets you down. Now you're in the dumps. A little country-western, maybe? It will offer sympathy since it's basically a soap opera set to music and deals with life's heartaches. Perhaps you need a dose of rhythm and blues or music in a minor key. Then somebody pays you a high compliment and suddenly you're full of energy, ready to accomplish great deeds. It's time for a marching band with a rousing drum cadence to get you out the door and on your way.

When I'm feeling rather lonely, I like my music loud so it can fill up the empty spaces in my soul. When I'm in a creative mood, I enjoy listening to a violin. You may substitute a guitar, a mellow saxophone, a flute, or the piano if one of those is more to your liking. Occasionally I feel kind of wild and crazy. That's when I plug in some soft rock with a good beat. I've never yet experienced a mood appropriate for either opera or serious jazz, although many people do.

The point of this discussion is that both music and life have incredible ranges of feeling tones and moods. Music would be boring if we had nothing but a steady diet of one single style or one singing group no matter how good they might be. I love classical music, especially Mozart. But if his compositions were all I could ever listen to, I'd eventually go bonkers.

The Creator gave us both the ability to think and to feel. It was a touch of genius. Our inner lives are rich and vital because we have minds and emotions. But it also makes things quite complicated. Unlike *Star Trek's* Spock, we don't act from pure reason and logic alone. Thoughts and feelings get tangled up inside us. We experience tremendous mood swings. It can be as exciting as riding a huge roller coaster, and as scary, too. Whee-e-e-e!

In a matter of moments I can go from being on top of the world to feeling so low my nose scrapes the pavement. It defies explanation. Apparently it's a natural part of being human. However, it can also leave me feeling wiped out, totally exhausted. While ups and downs are normal and healthy, they can wear down our bodies. I'd rather dig ditches all day and be physically tired than to be emotionally stressed.

Obviously everyone would prefer living "happily ever after." It's simply not a realistic goal. For one thing, since we're all related on this planet, when a child is hungry on another continent, my stomach can feel the pain thousands of miles away. When people in the Middle East live in turmoil, my heart has an unsettled feeling. When countless numbers of families on this earth are homeless, I can never feel quite comfortable even though I have a roof over my head. When war rages on the other side of our globe, I feel the pain along with its actual victims. In today's world, grief and sorrow are as much a part of our lives as joy and happiness.

It's a challenge for us to take seriously all the hurts and problems yet maintain a hopeful, positive attitude. That's exactly what God wants us to do. It's how Jesus lived. He cared deeply about the troubles of others but he also played with children, enjoyed a good meal, delighted in the company of friends, and marveled at the beauty of nature. He profoundly loved people, but he didn't worry and stew and fret. He knew what he could do to help, and he did it.

Unhappiness isn't necessarily bad. People can create marvelous works when they're feeling sad or depressed. It's the old "grain of sand in the oyster" routine. Many of the best authors, artists, and musicians led difficult and troubled lives. That doesn't mean we should go looking for problems. But when difficulties come, and eventually they will come to everyone, we can use these tribulations as sources of creativity. They can become the seeds of motivation to build a better world, the encouragement to try new ways, and the nudge we need to take risks we might never take if we remained at ease.

Mountaintop experiences are wonderfully stimulating. They aren't frequent; that is, they're uncommon and occur in the high country where people don't often venture. Spiritual highs often happen at places such as summer camps, retreats, and concerts. God periodically offers these for our inner refreshment, to give us a new perspective. But we are not intended to live there. How many cities have you seen on mountain peaks? Very few, I'll wager. It's too steep. There aren't many level building sites. The air is thin and the weather can be severe. In other words, they're great places for hikes and spiritual pilgrimages, but not for permanent residences.

Jesus once took three disciples and went into the mountains to pray. While they were there, the Transfiguration took place (Matthew 17:1-13). God made wonderfully visible the special and divine nature of Jesus. The disciples were understandably impressed and wanted to stay right there, to build a booth and set up camp. Jesus would have none of it. He led them back to the valleys below to be with people, to heal the sick, to feed the hungry, to comfort the sorrowing. Jesus demonstrated that joyful experiences are not just to be cherished by a few persons but are to be shared with many. Happiness slips right through our fingers when we try to hoard it. God asks us to pass it on, for in that process a miracle happens. We are blessed as well.

When we're in a funky, rotten mood and are feeling down, there are things we can do to start the climb back to where joys await us on the mountaintop. Just as climbers must have the proper equipment and practice the necessary skills, so also should we when it comes to things of the spirit. Here are some basic ways and preventative measures to nurture our joys and increase our happiness.

1. Focus on positive qualities and experiences. God makes it clear that you and I are special. We're children of God. When we get down on ourselves, we need to remember how much we're loved and the unlimited potential God has placed inside our minds and souls. We must learn to affirm the goodness in ourselves and in others. When things don't go quite right, don't label them "failures." Instead of "mistakes," let's call them "challenges to personal growth" or "stepping-stones to success." Especially do not see yourself as a failure. The power of positive thinking is not a gimmick. It's based on the truth that God made us unique and creative individuals and has destined us for eternity.

2. Choose a few trusted and loyal friends from among your acquaintances with whom you can pour out your soul. These must be people who freely and graciously allow you to be yourself. Keep a safe distance from opinionated and judgmental individuals. So you're a little bit grouchy? Your dearest friends will still love you. They'll accept without reservation all your feelings, from the height of joy to the depth of sorrow, from peacefulness to full-blown anger, from seriousness to total silliness.

3. Learn to be honest with that most important person of all—yourself. If you're not feeling particularly happy, admit it. That way you can deal openly and constructively with those emotions. Put your worries on the tabletop where you can see and sort them out. And always keep open the channels of communication between your head and your heart, between the rational and the emotional parts of your personality.

4. Use every spiritual resource you can lay your hands on. Worship regularly with the people of God. Sing or hum or

whistle hymns of faith. Who cares if people look at you funny? Even when you haven't a clue what words to use, pray. God will fill in the blanks and understand exactly what you mean. Read the Bible, especially books like the Psalms, Isaiah, the Gospel of John, the Letter to the Romans, or 1 Corinthians. Find someone who will listen as you share the insights you gain.

5. Reach out to others and let them reach back to you. Maintain a good balance between time alone and time spent with family and friends. When feeling lonely or sad, a loving and gentle touch always brings comfort. Hugs are the best tonics known to humanity. The miracle of a hug is that whenever you give one, you get one in return. When feeling sorry for yourself, it helps to stop thinking so much about poor old you and concentrate on the needs of others. Nothing can cure the blues faster than doing a kind deed for someone else. A blessing shared is a blessing received.

6. Be willing to admit that you need professional help when your emotional turmoil may be the result of more than normal mood swings. Don't hesitate to ask for help. There are times in all our lives when we can't find the answers by ourselves. Pastors, counselors, teachers and others have the intellectual tools, training, experience, and desire to serve in this capacity. If you have any doubts about your need for counseling, ask a parent or trusted friend to make an appointment for you and find out. Don't let anything block your opportunity for a rich emotional life. Feelings are essential ingredients in the recipe for happiness and wholeness.

Suppose for a moment you know how to play the piano but only a few keys, say those around middle C. It would certainly limit the songs you could play and the enjoyment you'd get. Even when performed to perfection, "Chopsticks" soon grows weary to the ears. Yes, there are more risks when your fingers use the entire keyboard. You stand a much better chance of making mistakes. But that's the way it is if you wish to experience music to the fullest. That's also how it is with our feelings. By expressing them all, you cannot be constantly happy.

It is, however, the doorway to experiencing inner warmth and richness.

Perhaps it will help if we realize happiness isn't earned; it's a gift from God, a wonderful bonus. It's given not because we're so wonderful but because God is so loving.

17

Is There a Class on How to Draw the Line?

Reflections of an "average kid"

I think I need a class on how and where to draw the line. I keep stepping over lines other people draw. I don't notice these lines like most adults can. Should I wear special glasses or something? In English class yesterday I guess I whispered too long after the bell rang because when I turned around the teacher was in my face. "You've stepped over the line once too often," she said. "It's detention for you." I should have hushed up then and there; but no, I had to ask a question. I didn't mean to be disrespectful, although that's apparently how it came out.

"What line?" I said. "I don't see any line." I ended up marching a straight line to the principal's office. I didn't pass "Go" and I certainly didn't collect two hundred dollars. I did get sent to jail, or something like it. I got a session of Saturday school added to my schedule. Sigh. Somebody needs to show me how to spot these invisible lines. I always thought they were imaginary, make believe, somebody's fantasy. But they must be real because they keep tripping me and getting me into trouble. Maybe they're drawn in disappearing ink. Or perhaps you can't see them until you're a certain age, something old like twenty-one or thirty.

There must be zillions of these lines. My parents talk about them all the time. Once I promised to mow the lawn, but I got involved in a computer game at my buddy's house and forgot to look at the clock. When I got home, the first words I heard were "I hope you have a good explanation, young man, because if you don't, you're way out of line! This time you've gone too far." I had to mow the lawn in the dark.

When I was a little kid, there were lots of places I couldn't go. I had to stay in our yard unless our next-door neighbor, Mrs. Thomas, invited me over. I wasn't supposed to play inside the car, and I had strict orders never ever to get in the high cupboard where the cleaning supplies were kept. One day I scooted an end table over, put the kitchen stool on top, and took a quick peek. I didn't find much; it wasn't worth the effort.

Now, however, I'm big enough to go almost anywhere I want, at least that's what I think. Other people seem to have different ideas; and that's where these mysterious lines come in. If they'd use chalk lines like we did when we played hop-scotch, that might help. I'm a visual person.

I decided to take the bull by the horns, as it were, and talk to my dad. "Hey, Dad," I asked. "Can we discuss how and where to draw the line?"

"Sure. Is this for a math assignment? I'll get a ruler and be right with you."

"No, Pop, that's not what I mean. I want you to help me figure out what I can and can't do, where I can go, how long I can stay out, that kind of stuff—you know, what the rules are for somebody my age."

"Oh, I understand; you want clarification of things like the chores we expect you to do, when the TV goes off on school nights, and which movies you can't go to at the theater."

"Right. I have this problem. I don't see some of those limits until it's too late. That may be partly because I kind of resent having so many. They make me feel boxed in, restricted, like you think I'm still a child."

"I know, Son, I felt the same way when I was your age."

"Well, what did you do about it?"

"That was a long while ago, but if I remember correctly, I talked to my parents and worked out a deal. They promised to be clearer about setting limits and explaining where they wanted the lines drawn. I agreed to try harder to stay inside the boundaries."

"Did it work?"

"Mostly. I was a normal kid, so I fudged sometimes. But from then on I appreciated more where they were coming from. Your grandpa and grandma weren't trying to spoil my fun. They really cared about me and my welfare, just like we care about you. I discovered an interesting thing. The better I obeyed the rules, the more flexible my folks became. Say, do you have a moment? I have a few words of parental wisdom to share."

"Sure, as long as it's shorter than your last lecture on being responsible about spending money."

"Agreed. Now then, you enjoy playing tennis, don't you?"

"You bet. I plan on making the varsity team some day."

"I hope you do. But what if a tennis court had no lines? Suppose it was nothing but a big slab of asphalt or concrete?"

"It would sure be hard to keep score. Nobody could tell if a ball was in bounds or out of bounds. Pretty soon everybody would be yelling and arguing and the games wouldn't be much fun."

"You're a perceptive and wise person, Son."

"Thanks, Dad. So far this pep talk's all right."

"Good. Have you noticed how almost every organized sport uses lines somewhere? Basketball has a court with lines all over. So does the ice for hockey."

"And football," I broke in. "It has yard markers, goal lines, hash marks, and end zones."

"That's correct. They help teams play fair and enjoy the

games. Without them, there'd be chaos. Well, it's basically the same with those unseen lines parents draw for their children. They're not meant to confine or stifle you but to keep you safe and out of harm's way. It's a method of giving you guidance. In sports there's freedom when people stay within the prescribed boundaries and follow the rules."

"Hey, Pop, this is starting to compute in my brain cells. Last week my Sunday school teacher was listing some of God's laws, like the Ten Commandments and the Golden Rule. He said almost the same things you're saying. God doesn't give us laws to frustrate or limit us but to set us free to live together in peace." I felt rather proud of myself for remembering the lesson. It was a first for me.

"Way to go, kiddo. You've probably also figured out that when you learn how to operate within the lines or rules of small things, you're ready to tackle bigger ones. This is an important step in maturation. Very soon you'll be facing critical decisions involving the use of drugs and alcohol."

"I hate to tell you this, Pop, but I already have. And I said 'No!' with an exclamation point."

"Great! Other major issues will come along soon involving prejudice, bigotry, honesty, integrity, your moral values, and your sexual standards. I'm glad to see you're preparing for these. They're tough but very important problems." I nodded in agreement. Dad went back to reading the evening paper, and I returned to my homework.

You might be interested to know I had one more lesson that day in learning where to draw the line. It involved a box of chocolate candy, the kind that melts in your mouth. They were small and tasted yummy. So I kept munching away until I finally looked down. The box was half empty. Suddenly my stomach had a funny feeling in it. I didn't care if I ever saw another piece of chocolate as long as I lived. When it comes to eating candy, those lines are not imaginary. Trust me on this. There are definite consequences when you go beyond them!

If I keep learning as much as I did that day, I won't need to take a class on drawing the line. I'll be able to teach it!

18

What If I Enjoy Being Rebellious?

I admit it. I was a rebellious kid and I rather enjoyed it. I liked kicking up my heels occasionally and causing a little ruckus. As I remember, it was pretty mild stuff. But it gave me a sense of self-determination and personal power. Once I switched salt in the shaker with sugar in the bowl. Nobody ever got hurt from this stunt, just surprised. Oh, I suppose it ruined my sister's breakfast cereal and got my parent's day off to a bad start. Around our house, I could never get away with anything because, other than my sister, I was the only kid living there. They always knew where to look when somebody pulled a prank.

The year I turned twelve, I decided I'd better try smoking. After all, I was nearly grown up. My experiment was a disaster, or depending on your viewpoint, a blessing. I stumbled on a box of Army rations that was probably ten years old. Among the stale crackers and other items was a pack of cigarettes. I sneaked out to the alley behind our garage and lit up. Two puffs later I started getting green around the gills. Three more puffs and the coughing and sputtering began. I inhaled once more and my stomach did a flip-flop followed by a flop-flip. I threw that cigarette to the ground, stomped on it with both feet, and haven't smoked anything since. Well, I once tried a cigar, thinking I'd look cool with a stogie in my mouth. I didn't. It made me look really dumb. I could feel those green gills coming back so I quit. I'd have been better off trying to smoke an old rubber tire.

Yes, I pulled my share of rebellious deeds as a young person. Thankfully my parents were patient and loving people with an excellent sense of humor. My brief forays into insubordinate behavior got the desired result: people noticed me. Granted, much of the attention wasn't particularly affirming. But at least the residents of that town knew I existed. I was also the proud owner of a wild wardrobe. Folks could spot me a mile away when I wore my florescent green pants, a red and black striped sweater, and my favorite shimmering gold shirt. I was a sight to behold, assuming you had dark glasses.

It's possible that whoever has authority to define terms decides whether a person is (a) unique and unusual, or (b) rebellious and defiant. What a youth might consider rambunctious but normal activity, a worn out and frazzled parent might view as full-scale rebellion. But consider the possibility that butterflies may think breaking out of the cocoon an act of rebellion. Perhaps hens think it's scandalous behavior when chicks peck their way out of eggs. After all, it ruins the eggshell and makes a mess in the nest. When adults become inflexible, rigid, and lose their ability to accept change, it basically forces preteens into a posture of rebelliousness—whether they want to be rebellious or not. Parents who don't know when "to go with the flow" will likely have kids who are frequently out of bounds.

Funny things can happen to people as they get older, besides gaining a few extra pounds and getting gray hair. They seem to need peace and quiet in ever-increasing amounts. They want greater control over their environment, including the people around them. And they try to reserve larger blocks of time for themselves. This poses no major problem. It's a natural part of the aging process, except (there's always an exception to every rule, isn't there?) when these adults happen to live under the same roof with youth.

Young teenagers may like their music loud, electronic, and with a driving beat; parents often prefer mellow strings and muted saxophones in the tradition of Lawrence Welk or elevator music. Young people think nights were made for slumber parties, watching three videos, and making kitchen raids; parents may have the notion that God made nights so people could sleep. We have here a since-the-beginning-of-history source of conflict waiting to erupt.

The key to the situation is how we handle it. If we lock horns, duke it out toe to toe, butt heads, or whatever phrase you use to describe confrontation, the outcome is quite predictable. Right or wrong, the bill payers will eventually emerge victorious, and those who need lunch money the next day and rides home from piano lessons and soccer practices will sooner or later see the wisdom of yielding. It may not be fair but, hey, we live in the real world. Then somewhere down the road that word "rebellious" sneaks into somebody's conversation, in a negative way, of course. "We can't do anything with Craig. He's just impossible—he's such a rebellious boy." This is usually accompanied by shoulder shrugging and a what-am-I-to-do look.

I'm here to say that rebelliousness is getting a bad rap, an undeserved reputation. It can be a very healthy and necessary ingredient in the process of maturation. Rebelliousness has a productive and wholesome dimension we ought not overlook. Perhaps we should assign it a different, less negative name like "assertiveness" or "striving for independence." Young people are not supposed to be carbon copies—make that faxes—of their elders. Society absolutely depends on youth for new ideas, creativity, and fresh insights. In other words, a bright future requires young people who are wholesomely rebellious.

At its highest level, rebellion is not hurtful. Frankly we need more pleasantly rebellious people, not fewer, including older models as well. Good rebellion isn't selfish or boastful; it doesn't put others down but lifts them up to new possibilities.

It strives to free not only the rebellious person but also to make space for others to grow. It can be a most helpful method for finding out what independence is all about, of standing up for one's own views, rights, and beliefs.

The Old Testament prophets were criticized by political and religious authorities for rebelling against both their leaders and God. Nothing was further from the truth. They were simply asserting and proclaiming what they knew deep within their souls to be the Word of God. If it was rebellion, so be it. But it was also truly inspired, divinely given, and wonderful.

Finding one's way safely through the preteen and teen years is not an easy task. There will be times when it seems as though it's not several years in duration but several decades! Hang in there—be true to yourself. You'll make a few wrong turns and go down a bunch of dead ends. Everybody has. But keep plugging. Cherish your own unique personality. Rejoice in your special gifts and abilities. And if you should be labeled "rebellious," hold your head high. You're in good company.

Even at my age I have a rebellious, stubborn streak. I'm proud of it. I'm not somebody else's clone. I'm a one-of-a-kind individual to whom God has given a distinct place and purpose. Others may think me stubborn and cantankerous, an old fool. Sometimes I probably am. I can accept that. I'm just trying to be true to myself, honest with others, and faithful to God. I hope you will be, too.

19

Why Did God Make Young People?

ost varieties of animals have a relatively short time of growth and development. Many go from infancy to maturity in a year or less. God could have chosen to do that with humans as well. It would have saved a lot of expense and worry on the part of parents. Instead, God chose to extend the human growing period for eighteen or more years. God and the angels may well have had a lively discussion about the wisdom of such a plan. "Why not cut it to just a couple of years," suggested an old angel with moss hanging from his wings. "How can you expect parents and offspring to get along with each other that long? Do you realize eighteen years is well over sixty-five hundred days and more than one hundred fifty thousand hours of togetherness?"

"Yes, I do," replied God. "I'm pretty good with numbers. If I can count every hair on people's heads, I should be able to figure that out. Any more comments or suggestions?"

"Well," offered a middle-aged angel, "you could at least do away with adolescence and have humans go directly from age ten to twenty. Why not skip that potentially awkward period?

It could be very tough on everybody concerned, including you."

"That's a risk I'm willing to take," answered God. "The role I've assigned to humans is so important that they'll need adequate time to learn everything. It's not just a matter of being able to walk and gather food and find a place to live. I want them to know how to talk and read and write, to be familiar with the whole of creation. I want them to be capable of inventing, exploring, teaching, traveling, philosophizing, and worshiping me. My hopes for them are so great they'll need that extra time—and perhaps even more—to grow into capable adults."

"Is it possible," a cluster of angels asked, "that you're expecting too much of these frail creatures? We've noticed that the first models have been a bit short on patience, quick to anger, and frankly don't show that much promise."

"Now just hold on to your halos. I'm not going to scale down my expectations. I'm going to help them reach for bigger and better things. My Spirit will constantly brood over them and nurture them."

"We predict you're in for some major disappointments, O Almighty One of the Universe. There are simply too many imperfections in these people. Sure, you gave them a large brain capacity. But we're afraid they won't know how or care enough to use it to the fullest."

"I've thought this all through," God said. "I don't intend for them to be perfect. I want them to be free, to be able to make their own choices, to love one another, and me too, out of the goodness in their hearts."

"Good luck, God. We're guessing in ten thousand years or so we'll be saying, 'We told you so.' Please reconsider, and get rid of adolescence!"

God stepped down from the throne, sat on a creaky, old rocking chair and said, "I feel a sermon coming on, so find a comfy cloud. I have solid reasons for creating young people. In fact, I'm absolutely certain they're going to be among my favorites. Here's how I've got it planned. I'm giving youth the most rapid growth rate of any age category. And that means they'll have by far the greatest potential in the human race. Plus it will give me teaching opportunities I'll never have with anyone else." God continued the monologue.

"This is exciting for me. I hope these youth will be fresh and pure—old enough to make wise decisions yet young enough to have hope for the future. To be honest, I shall need more people like them who are trusting, caring, and idealistic—people who haven't become disillusioned and given up on the possibility of peace on earth. I want joyful noises, and young teenagers are the ones to make them. They'll play energetic music—they'll sing and dance and shout. I figure soon enough there'll be plenty of pew sitters, hymn hummers, and guardians of the status quo. I won't be needing additional pillars in my church. Do you have any idea how hard it is to get them to change or move? I want young people who will remain open and flexible, who aren't afraid of novel ideas.

"Every so often in the history of that beautiful blue marble called 'Earth,' I'm going to plant seeds. I plan on nudging the nations and inspiring the people to do brand-new things. I shall renew everything from the tiniest organisms to the mightiest rulers. Because youth will not be set in their ways and because they'll be able to mold their wills to mine, they'll serve as my advance party for a new world. I'll put them in the front lines and give them responsibility for showing others the way, including those twice, thrice, or more their age. In their innocence they'll be equipped to overcome ancient antagonisms and they'll be capable of freeing people from prejudices and from a whole host of hurtful attitudes.

"Yes, I've made place of honor for young people in my scheme of things. So what if they eat everything in sight? They need plenty of fuel in order to have the energy required for doing my work. A few refrigerator raids aren't much compared to leading my people into a realm of abundance, equality, and justice.

"I trust they will understand I don't mean to dump a huge burden on their young shoulders. I'm giving them these tasks because I know they're capable of fulfilling them—that of all humans, they will be best able to retain their wonder, joy, and enthusiasm for life. It means they shall have to study hard and struggle mightily to discover the direction they're to go. I hope they'll remember I'll always be there with them. That's why I'm making young people!"

And all the angels said, "Amen!"